ACONCAGUA
HIGHEST TREK IN THE WORLD

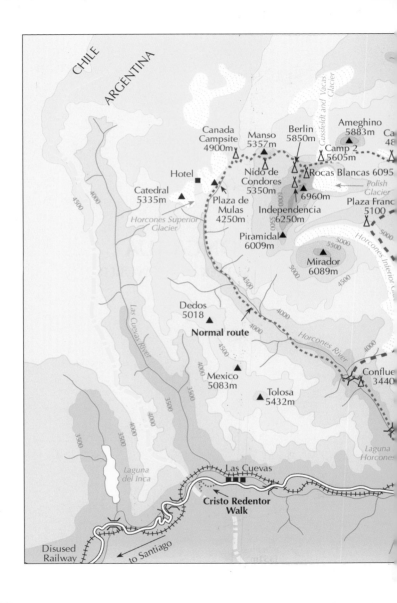

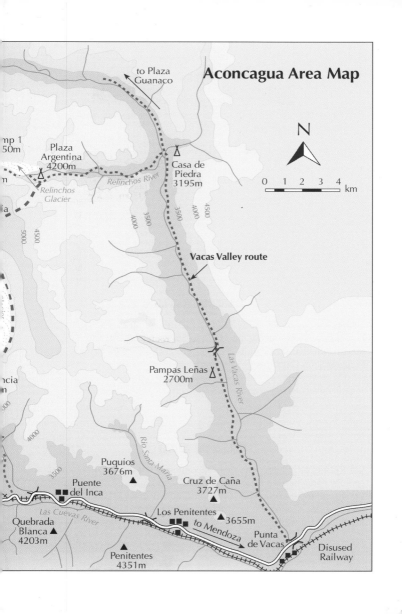

Aconcagua Area Map

N

0 1 2 3 4 km

to Plaza Guanaco

mp 1
50m

Plaza Argentina
4200m

Relinchos River

Casa de Piedra
3195m

Relinchos Glacier

4500

5000

4000

3500

3500

4000

4500

Vacas Valley route

Las Vacas River

ncia
n

Pampas Leñas
2700m

000

4000

Río Santa María

3500

Puquios
3676m

Cruz de Caña
3727m

Puente del Inca

Los Penitentes
3655m

to Mendoza

Punta de Vacas

Las Cuevas River

Quebrada Blanca
4203m

Penitentes
4351m

Disused Railway

I grew up in this city, my poetry was born between the mountain and the river, it took its voice from the rain, and like the timber, it steeped itself in the forests.

Pablo Neruda (Chilean poet)

Acknowledgements

Thanks are due to Sue Ryan for her patience and proof-reading, to Fergus Humphries for producing the maps, to Eduardo Depetris, Pablo Reguera, Sebastian Tetilla, Angel Tetilla, Marco Garrido Dasté, Pedro Marzolo, and to Professor John Gamble for identifying rocks.

About the Author

Jim Ryan is a civil engineer by profession. He has a particular interest in geology and a passion for the mountains. Aconcagua and its region made a significant impression on him on his first journey there as part of an expedition in 1999. Noting the lack of information on one of the world's great mountains he returned on two further expeditions to produce this book.

ACONCAGUA

HIGHEST TREK IN THE WORLD

Practical information, preparation
and trekking routes in the southern Andes

by
Jim Ryan

CICERONE

2 POLICE SQUARE, MILNTHORPE, CUMBRIA LA7 7PY
www.cicerone.co.uk

© Jim Ryan 2004
ISBN 1 85284 455 8
A catalogue record for this book is available from the British Library

Front cover: Rough trekking up the Relinchos Valley on the Polish Glacier route

CONTENTS

Map Key

	ridges
	roads
	route
	Vacas valley route
	normal route
	fresh water pipe
	national boundary
	tunnel
	railway
	glacier
	river
	water/lagoon
■	building
⊃⊂	bridge
●	town
▲	summit
⋀	camp
†	statue
⊕	airport

Contours

6500–7000m
6000–6500m
5500–6000m
5000–5500m
4500–5000m
4000–4500m
3500–4000m
3000–3500m
2500–3000m

PERU

BRAZIL

BOLIVIA

CHILE

PARAGUAY

Aconcagua
Mendoza

Santiago

ARGENTINA

URUGUAY

Buenos
Aries

Map of
South America

N

Falklands
(Malvinas)

Tierra del Fuego

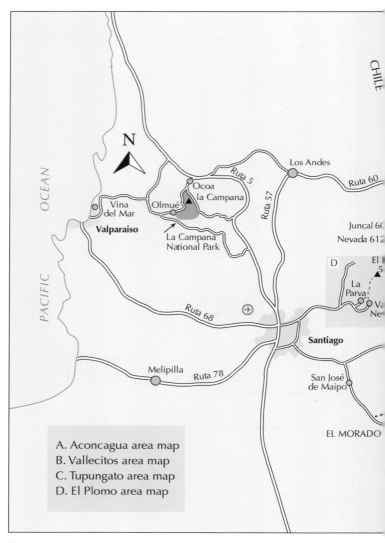

A. Aconcagua area map
B. Vallecitos area map
C. Tupungato area map
D. El Plomo area map

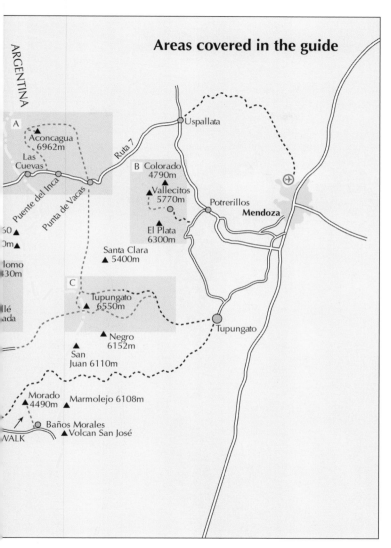

Areas covered in the guide

ARGENTINA

A
▲ Aconcagua
6962m

Las
Cuevas

Ruta 7

Puente del Inca

Punta de Vacas

Uspallata

B ▲ Colorado
4790m

▲ Vallecitos
5770m

Potrerillos

Mendoza

El Plata
6300m

50 ▲

0m▲

lomo
:30m

llé
ada

Santa Clara
▲ 5400m

C

Tupungato
▲ 6550m

▲ Negro
6152m

San
Juan 6110m

Tupungato

Morado
▲ 4490m ▲ Marmolejo 6108m

WALK

Baños Morales
▲ Volcan San José

A well-worn path through penitentes on the Normal route

FOREWORD

Aconcagua is not merely a mountain to me. It is my life. As a mountain guide I have summited Aconcagua too many times to recall.

Over two decades I have witnessed the number of climbers grow every year. In those two decades there has been a ten-fold increase in numbers, and the increase continues.

We who serve these climbers must adapt to cater for the numbers. A guidebook such as this will help in this regard, and it will improve our services to those who climb our mountain.

The degree of written material on Aconcagua is sparse. Until a few years ago there was no map of the mountain. R. J. Secor's guide has served us well for a decade, but a fresh new outlook is a breath of fresh air.

I welcome Jim Ryan's new book, and I am personally delighted to have assisted him in Argentina. His book is both accurate and interesting, and his maps and sketches are a revelation.

Sebastian Tetilla
Aconcagua guide, Mendoza

The glacier above Plaza Argentina with penitentes *in the foreground*

PREFACE

This book is intended primarily for the many thousands who travel each year to climb the highest peak outside the Himalayas – Aconcagua. The main concentration is the mountain itself. It is assumed that the traveller will fly into either Santiago or Mendoza.

For every eight who attempt the peak only two succeed. The majority fail as a result of altitude sickness or weather conditions, but also due to lack of preparation. A considerable section of the book is devoted to advice on acclimatisation and good preparations.

For those who prefer to acclimatise on mountains other than the primary goal, choices are offered near Mendoza (Vallecitos, 5770m) and Santiago (El Plomo, 5430m). Many will want to get to the Aconcagua Provincial Park and acclimatise there, and treks near and within the park are detailed with this in mind.

The intriguing story of the aircraft that crashed into a mountain en route from Mendoza to Santiago, and was swallowed in its glacier to re-emerge 50 years later, is documented. A special wilderness trek within Tupungato Provincial Park to the site of the crashed plane is outlined.

The central regions of Chile and Argentina have much to offer besides the mountains of the Andes. For those who are forced to abandon the climb due to problems with altitude or the weather, or who have time to spare, a range of other attractions is given.

To enable the traveller to gain the maximum from his experience information is included on geology, flora and fauna, customs and traditions, and the language itself. The cities of Santiago and Mendoza have had a special relationship since their foundations. Their history, people, customs and architecture will interest the traveller.

Finally, if the book has succeeded in convincing the reader to go to Aconcagua, the Useful Information section provides telephone numbers, Internet addresses, suggested places to stay and to eat, and other relevant data, as well as references to further reading, maps and other information.

Jim Ryan

View of Aconcagua up the Relinchos Valley

INTRODUCTION

THE ATTRACTION FOR CLIMBERS

The mountain of Aconcagua in the southern Andes is the highest peak in the world outside the Himalayas, and the highest of the seven continental summits after Everest. Of the seven summits, Aconcagua offers the climber the best value in terms of altitude gained for effort expended.

Over the past decade the pursuit of climbing and hillwalking has attracted more and more enthusiasts. Travel to far-off places has become less onerous. Mountain guides clog the Internet with advertisements of their adventure holidays. For those who tire of the commonplace, goals such as Kilimanjaro (Tanzania), Island Peak (Nepal) and Aconcagua are there to provide the adventure.

Aconcagua is seen as an essential stepping-stone for those with eyes on the big prize – Everest. However, the serious alpinist will have to rub shoulders with the adventurous trekker. The purist might contend that climbing in double plastic boots, with crampons and an ice axe, in temperatures of -20°C, can hardly be classified as a trek. Nevertheless, certain routes on Aconcagua require very little technical skill, and provide valuable high-altitude experience.

The area of South America in which Aconcagua is situated is quite civilised, transport is good, and there

Telephoto view of the summit from the roadhead

19

ACONCAGUA IN CONTEXT
THE HIGHEST MOUNTAINS OF THE SEVEN CONTINENTS

Continent	Mountain	Height (m/ft)
Asia	Everest	8850/29,035
South America	Aconcagua	6962/22,841
North America	Denali	6194/20,320
Africa	Kilimanjaro	5963/19,563
Europe	Elbrus	5633/18,481
Antarctica	Vinson Massif	4897/16,066
Oceania	Puncak Jaya	4884/16,023

is an established infrastructure for mountain access. There are no 'nasties' in the region, such as snakes, mosquitoes or wild cats. The people are friendly, food is great and language is not a particular barrier. The region has many other attractions, such as the vineyards of Chile and Mendoza, white-water rafting, the beach at Vina del Mar, rodeos and numerous other items of scenic and cultural interest.

Lest the impression be conveyed that Aconcagua is a bed of roses the following caution is appropriate. The mountain is bleak and harsh. The winds on Aconcagua can be unrelenting and the temperatures severe. The incidence of failure due to the effects of altitude and weather is particularly

THE 12 HIGHEST PEAKS OF THE AMERICAS

Mountain	Height (m/ft)	Country
Aconcagua	6962/22,842	Argentina
Ojos del Salado	688022,573	Argentina–Chile
Pissis	6779/22,242	Argentina
Mercedario	6770/22,212	Argentina
Huascarán	6768/22,206	Peru
Llullaillaco	6723/22,058	Argentina–Chile
Sin Nombre	6637/21,776	Argentina–Chile
Yerupajá	6634/21,766	Peru
Tres Cruces	6620/21,720	Argentina–Chile
Coropuna	6613/21,697	Peru
Incahuasi	6601/21,658	Argentina–Chile
Tupungato	6550/21,491	Argentina–Chile

high. Many climbers arrive unprepared for the cold and altitude, and repeat visits are common. Chile and Argentina are not third world countries, so costs are higher than in Nepal or Africa (but a fraction of those in Europe and North America).

There are no less than 164 peaks in the Himalayas that have greater altitudes than Aconcagua. In the Americas Aconcagua tops a list of 43 peaks, all in South America, ahead of Denali (McKinley) in Alaska.

Alpinists consider Aconcagua to be much more difficult than a large proportion of its Himalayan cousins due to its harsh environment, unpredictable weather, the dreaded Canaleta scree slope that must be overcome at 6800m, and the long distance to base camp. The relative distance of Aconcagua from the equator, compared to the Himalayas, is a factor in terms of weather and altitude. The further one travels from the equator the thinner the earth's atmosphere.

TWO TREKKING ROUTES

Every mountain has a diversity of routes to the summit. Aconcagua is no exception, and the majority are categorised as extremely difficult. However, there are two routes requiring minimal technical expertise, and these are described in detail in this book, with a brief reference to the route around to the north via Plaza Guanaco and the more advanced direct route up the Polish Glacier.

Over 70 per cent of all climbers take the **Normal route**, also known as the Horcones Valley route. The approach is from the south, 35km over a rough river valley to base camp at Plaza de Mulas. From here the route swings around to the east, over steep ground, eventually turning directly south to the summit.

The second popular trekking route is known as the **Vacas Valley route**, but is also commonly known as the Polish Glacier route. It is 42km from the road head to base camp at Plaza Argentina. Initially the direction is, like the Normal route, due north for 26km, then a left turn to the west, and a further 16km up the Relinchos river valley.

Both routes join high up the mountain, below a small ruined hut called Independencia, at 6250m.

Via the Normal route the summit will be visible for much of the journey to base camp, whereas on the Vacas Valley route it only comes into view at the left-hand turn after 26km. The average time (subject to acclimatisation) to the summit and back to the road head is 12 days via the Normal route, and 15 days on the Vacas Valley route.

At base camp (Plaza de Mulas) on the Normal route there is a hotel, fairly basic in comforts, but it does have a telephone link to the outside world. There are no such luxuries at Plaza Argentina. Nevertheless, the Vacas Valley route is less crowded and more picturesque. Consequently there is

Mules leaving Plaza de Mulas after unloading

more birdlife, and even the possibility of seeing some wild guanacos.

The Vacas Valley route is tougher and longer. However, for those not acclimatised, this pays dividends as you will be better prepared for summit day. The best option is to acclimatise on another mountain, such as at Vallecitos (between Mendoza and Aconcagua – see page 108) or El Plomo (between Santiago and Aconcagua – see page 135), then tackle Aconcagua via the Normal route.

LOCATION

Aconcagua is entirely within the Republic of Argentina, very close to the border with Chile. Halfway south to the middle of Chile and below the Tropic of Capricorn, it is in the province of Mendoza and the department of Las Heras.

The Aconcagua Provincial Park is immediately off the main road that links the cities of Mendoza in Argentina and Santiago in Chile. Of the 13 passes over the Andes between the two countries this is the only paved road. On the southern side of the road lies another of Mendoza's provincial parks – Tupungato Provincial Park.

The nearest village on the main road is Puente del Inca, which is 15km inside the Argentina/Chile border, 186km from Mendoza and 169km from Santiago. Between the starting points of the two trekking routes lies the village of Los Penitentes, a ski resort with a cable car (closed during the summer) up to the mountains.

PART I

ACONCAGUA – A PROFILE

Charles Darwin was the first explorer to examine the geology of the high Andes, and his 1835 sketch of the Puente del Inca rock formation remains a classic. The German geologist Walter Schiller, however, is recognised as the father of Andean geology, perhaps only surpassed in recent times by the Argentinean Victor Ramos.

The geological deposits of Aconcagua can be divided into three periods:

- base sedimentary rocks
- higher volcanic rocks
- glacial and alluvial deposits

The base sedimentary rocks range in age from Carboniferous, through Permian, Triassic and Jurassic into the Cretaceous period, dating back approximately 100 to 300 million years.

The base rocks under the Vacas Valley are the oldest, and these Carboniferous slates can be seen on the high ground east of Puente del Inca, and above Los Penitentes. The Permian rocks that form the sides of the Vacas Valley are the second oldest. Up at the south face of Aconcagua, near Plaza Francia, red Jurassic and early Cretaceous limestones are visible at the western base. On the walk in to Confluencia a grey limestone boulder field will be passed. These boulders have come down from a Jurassic formation high on the mountain.

Tectonic plate movements have lifted up and twisted these base rocks, so that fault lines and dramatic folds are common. Volcanic activity accompanied the tectonic plate movements, so that these older deposits support extensive masses of volcanic lavas and ashes of more recent date.

The convergence of the oceanic plate and the South American plate,

Rock stratification in the Horcones Valley

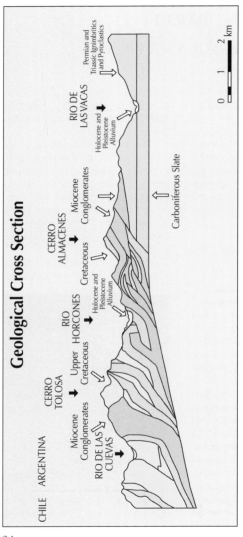

Geological Cross Section

CHILE ARGENTINA

RIO DE LAS CUEVAS
Miocene Conglomerates

CERRO TOLOSA

Upper HORCONES Cretaceous

RIO HORCONES
Holocene and Pleistocene Alluvium

CERRO ALMACENES
Cretaceous

Miocene Conglomerates

RIO DE LAS VACAS
Holocene and Pleistocene Alluvium

Permian and Triassic Ignimbritics and Pyroclastics

Carboniferous Slate

0 1 2 km

estimated at 90 to 100mm per annum, has resulted in a number of major earthquakes in the region, notably in 1861 (which destroyed Mendoza) and even as recently as 1985, with an epicentre in Valparaiso.

Metamorphic heat has transformed some of the sedimentary rocks. Great mountains of trachyte rise from the sedimentary base. In his treatise titled *Der Vulcan Aconcagua* (1884) the German naturalist and climber Paul Gussfeldt postulated that there was once likely to have been a crater on the south summit.

The predominant rock found on Aconcagua is grey with black particles. It is not unlike sandstone, but has been positively identified as a volcanic andesite. This same rock outcrops on the summit, and can be seen on many of the scree slopes. Above the Berlin camp, below Rocas Blancas, on the west and north sides, there are areas of thermal clay, yellowish in colour and containing traces of sulphur. Thus Aconcagua is essentially an extinct or an uplifted volcano, perched on top of a sedimentary base.

The river valleys south of the mountain contain deep deposits of gravel from four periods of glaciation and from natural erosion. Ice and frost on the mountain account for much of the latter. In the Horcones Valley these glacial and alluvial deposits are up to 5m deep, cut through by the river. The Horcones and Vacas rivers have a high discharge and flow very fast in the summer season, as snow and ice higher up melts. The water is dark red in colour, as it conveys its load of suspended solids that are deposited in the valleys below.

Detail of the mountain's penitentes

TOPOGRAPHY

The central Andes is divided into four north-south cordilleras. Immediately west of Mendoza is the relatively low **Precordillera**. This is the mountain range that blocks a view of the high peaks from the city. Beyond it to the west is the **Frontal Cordillera**, including peaks such as Vallecitos (5770m) and El Plata (6300m). The **Principal Cordillera** includes Aconcagua (6962m), Tupungato (6550m) and El Plomo (5430m). Finally, west of Santiago is the **Coastal Cordillera** that has mountains such as La Campana (1880m) and Roble Alto (2198m).

From the Vallecitos area there is a mountain range that stretches across in a northeast-southwest direction from the Frontal Cordillera towards Tupungato in the Principal Cordillera. This range is known as **Cordón del Plata**, and includes El Plata (6300m) and Vallecitos (5770m).

The climbing history of Aconcagua documents many attempts at finding a route to the summit, via the various valleys, over glaciers, and so on. This provides some insight into the difficult terrain in the area; there are no fewer than 13 peaks with an altitude over 5000m encircling Aconcagua.

The jagged appearances of the mountains at high level contrast with the smooth river valleys below. Sharp mountain features mellow into scree slopes that sweep down to the rivers. Landslides are common in these valleys.

There are five main glaciers in the Aconcagua area. The most significant is the Polish Glacier that covers the

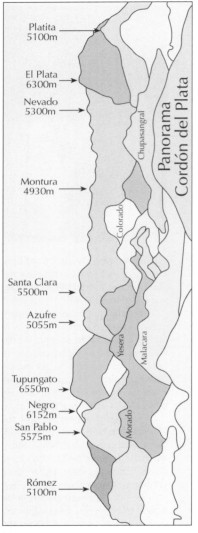

eastern side of the mountain. Next in importance is the Horcones Inferior Glacier, which swings around from behind the Mirador mountain (directly south of Aconcagua) to run down to within a few kilometres of the campsite of Confluencia. This glacier, hardly recognisable from the air because it is covered in scree, is up to 20m in depth. A slowly moving mass of ice, it groans and squeaks as it slides down the valley.

Minor glaciers abound on Aconcagua. Some, like the Horcones Inferior Glacier, are covered in rocks and scree, tens of metres thick, slowly moving down the valleys. Others are white and covered with *penitentes*, a particular feature of the region. These ice spikes range from a few centimetres to as high as 4m. Caused by the very cold winds on the mountain, the *penitentes* are set out in a linear pattern, generally with approximately half a metre between spikes. Wonderful to photograph, particularly when they are white, they present a formidable barrier to the climber.

The Horcones Valley approach has a pleasant area near the road head that provides a 'picture postcard' view of the mountain. With the harsh white outline of the peak in the background Laguna Horcones is a green, lush picnic point 3km from the road. Sightseers will often stop at the park entrance

The Horcones Inferior Glacier is up to 20m thick in places

and walk the 3km away from the noise of the busy traffic to the tranquillity of the water's edge.

FLORA AND FAUNA

During the summer low-growing cactus and other wildflowers provide minimal ground cover in as far as Confluencia on the Horcones Valley route and as far as Plaza Argentina on the Vacas Valley route. There are small areas of grass, more frequent in the Vacas Valley, and it is most likely that cows will be grazing in the Vacas Valley (Valley of Cows).

Orchids and calandrinias will be plentiful in the spring and early summer. In November the viola is just coming into flower.

The distinct probability is that, on a trek to the summit, no live animals – not even a rodent – will be seen.

There will be an abundance of small birds, particularly on the Vacas Valley route, but rarely larger birds, and few of any type above the base camps. Small lizards will often be seen, scurrying in the rocks in the Vacas Valley below Pampa de Leñas.

Yellow orchids amidst a sea of calandrinias near Confluencia

Calandrinias

The condor of South America is a very large bird that hovers in the sky. Another bird of prey, *carancho andino*, has the same features as the condor (but with a degree of white on the wings and rear body) and hovers

Violas emerge from the winter and prepare to bloom

too, but is much smaller and often mistaken for a condor. A condor has a wingspan of over 3m; its wing ends are distinctly serrated and have a band of silver feathers. In between the condor and the *carancho* in size is the *jote cabeza negra* (or, if it has a red head, *jote cabeza roja*). This is also a black vulture that hovers, but has no white feathers.

The small birds that hop around the lower campsites are known as *testes*. These are finches, either the sierra (*cometinos gayi*) or greater yellow (*chirihue dorado*). Both have a dark head and a yellow breast. Scraps of food will entice them into photo range.

A bird that will be heard though seldom seen is the *perdicita*, the Andean partridge. It has mottled wings, a grey head and orange legs, and a call that could be likened to

The Sierra finch – a common visitor to campsites

The inquisitive truca of La Campana National Park

a pump that needs oil. On the El Plomo trek there will be many birds at Piedra Numerada, including the noisy *perdicita*. The brown birds with grey breasts and a golden scalp are monk-headed tyrants (*dormilonas fraile*).

The red fox and the guanaco are the only animals that might be seen, the guanaco only in the Vacas Valley. The red fox of the Andes (*dusicyon culpaeus*) is the same size as a domestic dog, its red fur generally grey-white on its back. The fox will seldom be seen during the daytime, but may wander around the lower campsites at night, searching for scraps. Beware: it can transmit rabies.

Guanacos (*llama guanicoe*) are relatives of the common South American domesticated llama. They have a curled yellow fur with a white belly. Roaming in small herds, they are very nervous animals that avoid human presence. Guanacos are amazingly agile, and upon detecting potential predators will run high into the hills. The herd will generally consist of several females and their young, and one dominant male. They have a high-pitched call, and their droppings are similar to those of sheep.

Lizard (*Liolaemus nigromaculatus*) in Tupungato Provincial Park

A guanaco

29

ANCIENT HISTORY

The ancient history of southern Chile and Argentina is not well documented. Humans are thought to have crossed from North to South America approximately 15,000 years ago, reaching down as far as Tierra del Fuego some 10,000 years later.

Tribes such as the Araucanos, Aymaras and later the Wari are believed to have been early inhabitants of Chile before the Incas. The Mapuche people lived south of Santiago and dominated most of Argentina.

The Incas

From sometime in the later part of the 15th to the middle of the 16th century the Incas took control of northern Chile, but were repelled from Argentina by the Mapuche.

There is evidence that the Incas held the mountains in high regard, that they climbed them and offered sacrifices to their gods from them. In 1947 the remains of a guanaco were discovered between the north and south ridge of Aconcagua. It was thought that it was brought there as a sacrifice, and the ridge has been known since as Cresto del Guanaco.

Mummies have been uncovered on this and other peaks. On the nearby peak of Cerro Piramidal, for instance, the mummified remains of a young girl have been discovered, and another was unearthed on top of Llullaillaco (6723m). On the summit of El Plomo (5430m), overlooking

Museum's archaeological impression of the Aconcagua mummy

Museum's record photo of the excavation of the Aconcagua mummy

the city of Santiago, there is an Inca altar and a burial site where the mummified remains of a child were discovered in 1954.

In Mendoza's Parque General San Martin (where you must go to obtain a permit to climb Aconcagua) there is a small natural history museum, Museo Cornelio Moyano. Housed here until relatively recently (now in the Criant nearby) were the remains of a mummified body found at 5300m on the southwestern side of Aconcagua.

Advent of the Spanish conquistadors

The Spanish conquests of the Incas by Pizarro in the middle of the 16th century were to change the history of the entire western side of South America. In 1520 Magellan had discovered the straits that enabled passage between Spain and Asia. Spanish expeditions from the north eventually led to the invasion by Valdivia, the great Spanish general, who founded the city of Santiago.

In 1561 the then captain general of Santiago, General Mendoza, sent an expedition over the Andes where the city of Mendoza was founded, and named after him. Thus Mendoza became a province of Santiago, despite the enormous obstacle of the Andes in between. Cultural and commercial ties between the two cities that developed in the 16th century remain today.

Decades of conflict followed with the Mapuche, and General Valdivia

was killed by them in 1553. Then, in 1641, a treaty was reached leaving the Mapuche autonomous below the River Biobio. Only as late as the 19th century did the Mapuche integrate to become part of Chile.

Spanish colonial rule followed in both countries until the early part of the 19th century, when Napoleon invaded Spain. The consequent uncertainty ended with Chile declaring independence in 1810, and Argentina following in 1816. It was not until 1818, however, that the great heroes of Chile, José de San Martin and Bernardo O'Higgins, formally created the new nation, following the final defeat of the Royalists.

Mendoza suffered a severe earthquake in 1861. With the epicentre in

The statue of General San Martin in Mendoza

its heart the devastation was enormous, and thousands were killed. Relief for the homeless came from around the globe and helped in the rebuilding of the city. An earthquake on the Chilean side accounted for 20,000 deaths in 1906. Measured at 8.6 on the Richter scale, its epicentre was in Valparaiso.

RECENT HISTORY

Both countries have had colourful recent pasts. Chile's wealth was initially built on copper, silver and nitrates. Argentina's economy was largely centred on cattle and sheep. Nowadays wine production is a relatively new source of wealth for both countries, Chile producing more than Argentina. It is interesting to note that Aconcagua is one of the five demarcated wine regions of Chile.

The production of maize, soya and other crops continues to be significant for Argentina, and Argentinean beef has a worldwide reputation. Garlic is an important Mendocino product. South of Mendoza there are a number of small oil wells.

Chile has courted with socialism: in 1886 with President Balmaceda, in 1920 with President Palma, and finally in 1970 with Salvador Allende. A workers-supported military coup brought Juan Peron to power in Argentina in 1946. Military rule continued until after President Galtieri took on the British in his ill-fated invasion of the Falklands in 1982.

In 1985 Mendoza was rocked by another earthquake, but the damage to the relatively new low-rise buildings was not significant. Valparaiso was the epicentre of Chile's most recent earthquakes in 1971 and 1985.

A vineyard near Santiago

Santiago's modern architecture

Chile has a population of nearly 15 million, of which the Mapuche account for nearly one million. The majority of the population is mestizo, a mix of Hispanic and Indian. By contrast the vast majority of Argentina's 36 million people are of European descent. Many original Mendocinos (citizens of Mendoza) came from Italy, and the significance of their ancestry is marked by a major festival in March every year, centred around Plaza Italia. The people who live and work in the mountain region, on either side of the border, have distinctive Indo-European features.

Chile suffered under the regime that followed Allende, and many fled the country. Since the return to democracy there has been a gradual return of these exiles, many from Spain, bringing with them new ideas that have sparked a revitalisation of Chilean culture. This is most clearly seen in its modern architecture, and Valparaiso's school of architecture has achieved world standing.

Chile's current domestic problems are marked by increasing claims for land rights by the Mapuche, who claim that many millions of hectares of traditional Mapuche lands were taken by the government and sold.

The United Nations' Index of 2001 on poverty ranked Argentina in 34th place and Chile in 39th place. Whilst the centres of cities such as Buenos Aires and Santiago display affluence there is deep poverty in the countryside, particularly in Chile.

The collapse of the Argentinean economy in 2001/2002 was a turning point for this once great nation. Inflation during that year reached

Country scene in Chile

300 per cent, unemployment soared, and political unrest was rife. Within a brief two years Argentinean society had tumbled from its perch as the most

The statue of Christ the Redeemer on the border

affluent in South America to one that resembled its poorer northern neighbours. The economy has since steadied, and confidence is gradually being restored.

Argentinean–Chilean relationships

These neighbours have been close to war on a number of occasions, all related to border disputes. Queen Victoria arbitrated between them in 1902, Queen Elizabeth II in 1977. It was not until the 1990s that the two presidents made a lasting peace.

The enormous statue on the border – Christ the Redeemer (Cristo Redentor) – was erected by both countries as a sign of peace after the 1902 treaty. The area around the statue, on the original old road, was a particular point of dispute, so that to erect it on the agreed border highlighted its significance. The inscription on its plaque reads 'These mountains will fall before the peace between our countries is broken'.

Although the border has been the main source of dispute there has always been a good relationship between the cities of Santiago and Mendoza. The proximity of Mendoza to Santiago, rather than to its national capital, Buenos Aires, and the excellent road and air connections, are undoubtedly factors in this relationship. The Spanish spoken in Mendoza is more akin to Chilean Spanish than to Argentinean Spanish. A trip to the seaside, for Mendocinos, has always been via Santiago to Vina del Mar.

The village of Las Cuevas

THE BORDER AT ACONCAGUA

An Argentinean–Chilean treaty in 1881 agreed that the border would run over the highest peaks of the cordillera. Aconcagua lies to the east of this natural frontier. Military security has dictated, until relatively recently, that no maps of the region would be distributed.

CLIMBING HISTORY

The mountain pass over the Andes to the south of Aconcagua, now Route 7 from Santiago to Mendoza, was an ancient Inca trail, and the mountain is clearly visible from here. In 1818 José de San Martin and Bernardo O'Higgins used this pass to bring the Great Army of the Andes down into Chile to defeat the Spanish.

Charles Darwin visited the region in 1835, and is reputed to have experienced earth tremors during his excursion ashore from the *Beagle*. Paul Gussfeldt, a German climber and naturalist, made an unsuccessful attempt at the summit in 1883.

In late 1896 the Englishman Edward Fitzgerald led a serious expedition. In his team were the Swiss climber Matthias Zurbriggen and another English climber, Stuart Vines. They set off from the mountain pass up the Vacas Valley, decided this was an impossible route, and returned to try the Lower Horcones Valley. Concluding that the south face was too difficult they returned to Confluencia and proceeded up what is now the Normal route.

After many weeks on the mountain Zurbriggen arrived on the summit on 14 January 1897. A month later

Vines and an Italian porter named Nicola Lanti summited. Fitzgerald, unfortunately, never made it due to altitude sickness. He did, however, write a detailed account of his expedition, listing the conditions he encountered, the flora and fauna he had identified. This treatise remains today as an important document, not only in relation to Aconcagua, but also to early studies of the Andes.

In March 1934 four Polish climbers – Konstanty Narkievitcz-Jodko, Stefan Osiecki, Wictor Ostowski and Stefan Dasyinski – ascended via the Polish Glacier. Part of a six-man party, they had ascended via the Vacas and Relinchos valleys. Severe weather had kept the party pinned on the glacier at 6300m until they could make the decisive thrust to the summit. The Polish Glacier is named after them.

A French team travelled up the Lower Horcones Valley in 1954, and established a campsite (now known as Plaza Francia) under the south face. One month later six of the team reached the summit. It was late in the evening and they descended via the Normal route. However, they were lucky to be picked up by other climbers, and they suffered severe frostbite.

The Argentinean army controlled the area until 1980, imposing many restrictions. In 1983 the area was declared a provincial park, opening the way to increased popularity. Argentina has 22 national parks, yet although Aconcagua attracts many thousands of visitors every year it has not yet been elevated to national park status.

During the first open season in 1983, 346 people climbed the

The Polish Glacier on the eastern side of Aconcagua

The hotel at Plaza de Mulas

mountain. In the 2002/2003 season this had risen to 3800 climbers and 2132 low-level trekkers, more than a 10-fold increase. The mountain inevitably suffered under this traffic. In 1990 the government decided on a programme of cleaning and maintenance; mules were taken as high as Independencia to remove rubbish, and strict procedures were adopted to keep the mountain clean, with refuse sacks being issued to all climbers.

In 1992 the hotel was constructed near Plaza de Mulas. The worrying incidences of rockfall, particularly one that destroyed 10 tents, forced the authorities to move Plaza des Mulas in 1997. Confluencia was also moved in 1999 to control pollution.

There are various recordings of ascents and descents over the years.

The fastest ascent, from Plaza de Mulas to the summit, has steadily decreased from 9 hours in 1987 to 5 hours 45 minutes in 1991 (by a German by the name of Porsche!). The fastest descent was by parachute in 1985 when A. Steves of the French Air Force came down in 25 minutes. In 1991 and 1992 records were further set for an ascent and descent in one day via the Normal route and the Polish Glacier route.

TREKKER/CLIMBER PROFILES

A great diversity of people go to the Andes to climb Aconcagua. The vast majority – nearly 60 per cent – are young males in their 20s or 30s. However, the mountain attracts climbers from younger than 15 to

Trekkers in the Horcones Valley

those in their 70s. Over 10 per cent are female.

Of the nationalities represented Argentineans are obviously the most numerous. A significant number of local Argentineans obtain permits to trek but not to climb the mountain. However, the majority of other nationals come with the sole purpose of climbing. They come from all corners of the globe, with North Americans as the biggest contingent.

Interestingly Germans, British, French and Spaniards outnumber Chileans.

WEATHER ON ACONCAGUA

The most predictable aspect of the weather on Aconcagua is its unpredictability! During the summer months it will generally be very windy all the time. Out of the wind, down in the valleys, the temperature will be as high as 27°C at midday and as low as 3°C at midnight. At top camp the temperature will fall to at least -15°C – possibly -30°C – at night. In the middle of the day on the summit the temperature could range from -25°C to +15°C. During the summer it will be quite cold on the mountain in the morning until the sun rises. After 6pm sunset will come quickly, and the temperature will drop sharply within a short period.

The predominant winds in the central Andes come from the west or

The winds whip up on the mountain above Plaza de Mulas

A storm over Aconcagua contrasts with tranquillity at Horcones

southwest. As they rise over the mountains their velocity increases. In summer precipitation is rarely in the form of rain, usually snow. During the day, therefore, winds whip through the valleys, and at night ice-cold winds come down from the mountaintops. An important feature of the weather on Aconcagua is the wind-chill factor. When the wind is particularly strong and cold this can have the effect of lowering the temperature, from leeward side to windward side, by as much as 15°C.

The region is subject to *El Niño*, a summer phenomenon in the southern hemisphere that can dramatically alter the weather. The cold Antarctic waters that flow northwards along the South American coast are deflected to the west. Warmer seas, with increased evaporation, means heavy rain. In

January 1998 Buenos Aires was hit with 70mm of rain in a few hours, causing extensive flooding.

El Niño, however, is as likely to influence dry weather as wet weather, and there have been periods of extreme drought. On the western side of South America in 1998, for instance, there was no rain during winter or spring, causing severe drought. *El Niño* tends to occur in a pattern of once every five years, making 2008, 2013 and so on potentially vulnerable.

The Aconcagua peak has its own microclimate. The weather can be pleasant in the central Andes whilst a storm is raging up on Aconcagua. Electric storms during the summer are not uncommon. Occasionally the weather will produce a mushroom of cloud over the summit, with severe winds and driving snow.

Weather watching is a particular expertise of the local guides, and much of their conversation revolves around this topic. Winds from the south are a sign of good weather, those from the north or west the opposite. The guides will know the normal barometric pressure at each campsite and will be alerted by changes in the barometer.

On all the Andean peaks the daily pattern tends to an early clearance of cloud that may provide clear weather until midday. In the early afternoon clouds usually appear, engulfing the summit by mid to late afternoon, then clearing again as night falls. Summiting at midday is therefore good forward planning.

During the 2001/2002 season, from 24 to 30 December, the wind blew down the Horcones Valley from the north. A blizzard greeted new arrivals at Plaza de Mulas on 1 January. Many of them had left Confluencia in T-shirts and shorts, and were caught unawares. Meanwhile, up on the mountain there were no successful summits for five days, and only nine successful attempts in the succeeding two days. Hundreds of climbers went home disappointed. Determined climbers descended to recover, recalling six nights of -26°C.

In early January 2003, there was snow on the summit, and the Canaleta was relatively easy to climb with crampons. Within a few days the snow was gone and the Canaleta scree had returned to its usual loose nature. The winds whipped up, gusting to over 100kmph; wind-chill reduced temperatures by 15°C, but the severe

Plaza de Mulas under snow

WEATHER IN SANTIAGO AND MENDOZA

Month	Max/min T (°C)		Monthly rainfall (mm)	
	Santiago	Mendoza	Santiago	Mendoza
January	29/12	32/16	3	29
February	29/12	30/15	3	33
March	27/10	27/13	5	28
April	23/8	23/8	13	13
May	18/6	18/7	64	10
June	14/4	14/3	84	9
July	15/3	14/2	76	8
August	17/4	17/4	56	5
September	19/6	19/7	31	13
October	21/8	21/10	15	17
November	22/9	27/11	8	18
December	28/11	30/15	5	20

During the summer it will generally be a little warmer and more humid in Mendoza than across the mountains in Santiago. Whereas there will be virtually no chance of rain during the Santiago summer, in Mendoza the summer is not only the warm season, but also the wet season. A monthly summer rainfall of only 20mm to 30mm is nevertheless extremely small. Santiago has more than double Mendoza's rainfall, but all during winter.

winds only lasted a few days. When they abated the weather was ideal for climbing, with the temperature on the summit in the mid teens (°C).

GETTING THERE

The climbing season on Aconcagua runs from mid November to mid March, during the South American summer. In mid November it is springtime, but the snow on the Andes is deep, and the weather unpredictable. The various camps are being set up, and the arrieros are coming up from the lowlands. December and January is high season, with 80 per cent of annual climbing activity; the weather is best from mid December to early February. By mid March the summer has ended, the frequency of storms in the Andes increases, and those who serve the climbers are packing up for another year.

At the height of the season the base camps are crowded, mules are nearly all pre-booked, accommodation at Los Penitentes and Puente del Inca is full, the cost of a permit is high, and an extra premium is added to almost everything. On the Normal route there are many climbers vying for clean snow to melt, and sanitation suffers.

To climb outside the designated season nevertheless requires a permit. In order to discourage climbers when there is no emergency rescue, no ranger control and no services on the mountain, the authorities impose the high season rate.

The best balance between avoiding the crowds and getting good weather can be found over the two-week period before Christmas, or during the last week in January and the first week in February. This avoids

A mule train en route out of Confluencia

43

the surge of people who want to celebrate Christmas then leave for the climb. A review of the statistics shows – for some strange reason – a dip in the numbers who arrive in the last week in January.

Mendoza is very busy in late February and early March during the grape harvest. The great wine festival takes place during the first week in March, when the city is filled with visitors. Accommodation will be difficult to procure, and many of those working on Aconcagua may return to the lowlands to help with the harvest and join in the festivities. However, if accommodation is secure, the carnival atmosphere can provide an exhilarating finish to an expedition.

TREKKER NUMBERS

Official figures of trekkers on the mountain, calculated by taking an average over seven seasons (year-to-year variation does not seem to be significant)

Month	Week	% annual trekkers
November	3	1.0
	4	2.3
December	1	4.0
	2	5.8
	3	10.0
	4	12.6
January	1	14.0
	2	13.0
	3	11.1
	4	8.2
February	1	9.1
	2	5.0
	3	2.3
	4	1.0
March	1	0.5
	2	0.1

THE INWARD JOURNEY

The Aconcagua road head lies roughly midway along the main road from Mendoza to Santiago. However, since you have to obtain a permit in person at Mendoza, this city is the most convenient starting point.

International flights do not land in Mendoza, and the nearest international airport is Santiago (35 minutes' flight away), or Buenos Aires (one-and-a-half hours' flight away). The following airlines operate into Chile and Argentina:

- Aerolineas Argentinas (National Airline of Argentina)
- LAN Chile (National Airline of Chile)
- Varig (National Airline of Brazil)
- Iberia (National Airline of Spain)
- American Airlines
- United Airlines
- British Airways

It pays to take some time in planning the flights, and examining cost alternatives. An experienced global travel agent can reduce flight costs by up to a third.

From Europe there is a variety of choices of air route. The traveller may opt to fly into London's Heathrow to

The flight into Santiago from the north swings around Aconcagua presenting an excellent view of the mountain and the Horcones approach

connect for a flight for Brazil. Alternatively there is the route via Madrid direct to Santiago or Buenos Aires. Finally, there is the option of flying to the USA and then flying to Santiago or Buenos Aires.

It is sensible to compare the three alternatives for cost and time delays at the various airports. It is most likely that the London–Brazil–Santiago route will provide the best combination in terms of time and cost. A booking via the South American airline (Varig, in the case of Brazil) is likely to be considerably less expensive than a booking for the same journey via a European airline. Flights via Madrid are generally with Iberia, Spain's national airline, or Lanchile, the Chilean national airline. In the past the South American airlines have tended to insist on full payment for the

flight three months in advance – not the practice with European or American airlines. A booking via a global agent may, however, obviate this requirement.

It is most likely that the choice of travelling from Europe via the USA will prove the longest in time and the most expensive.

Sao Paulo, in Brazil, is a common stopover en route from Europe. The flight from Sao Paulo or Madrid to Santiago circles around Aconcagua before descending to land. The view from the aeroplane can be quite spectacular – try for a seat on the

Survival tip

Buses and trains in both Argentina and Chile run on time.

45

right-hand side of the plane. Flying from Buenos Aires to Mendoza, conversely, provides no view of the Andes.

From North America there are direct flights to Santiago from New York, Los Angeles, Dallas and Miami. Whether it is a direct flight or one with a stopover (Lima is popular), the flight path is generally along the Pacific coast, with a view of the Andes out of the right side window.

USA passport carriers must pay a reciprocity tax on landing in Santiago, and in 2003 this was set at $100. There is an additional tax of $18 on leaving from Santiago. In Buenos Aires USA passport carriers are taxed $23.50 on departures.

Some parties land in Santiago, then travel by bus over the Andes to Mendoza, stopping off to look at the mountain en route, and returning to the Andes after a day or so in Mendoza. The road journey is a round trip of 540km, which can be rather tedious, especially if all it achieves is a brief look at the mountain. A stop to trek up to the statue of Christ the Redeemer, or to watch river rafting, will be welcomed.

VISAS, PASSPORTS AND PERMITS

Visas are not required from any Western or first world country to enter either Chile or Argentina.

For Chile, visas are required from Russia, a number of Central American countries, Korea and former communist countries. In both countries the traveller's passport must have at least six months' validity remaining, and generally entry to the country is restricted to 90 days.

The first view of Aconcagua from the main Santiago-to-Mendoza road can be exhilarating

Outside the permit office in Mendoza

There are rumours that Argentina may move to protect the livelihood of its guides by forbidding foreign guides from operating in the country. If you are going as leader of a group it may be worth considering that you are not working, but on holiday too (foreign guides have to pay the permit fee, but registered Argentinean guides are exempt).

Expect to be delayed for some time at the border crossing whilst passports and luggage are checked, and also to pay a few dollars to a bureaucratic official who may insist on a more thorough luggage examination. This petty corruption is more likely on the Argentinean than on the Chilean side.

Before entering Aconcagua Provincial Park you will need a permit. These are issued in Mendoza, at the Direccion de Recursos Naturales Renovables in Parque General San Martin. You must appear in person, fill in forms and show your passport.

COST OF PERMITS FOR ACONCAGUA PROVINCIAL PARK (2003)				
Season	**Dates**	**Climbing**	**Long trek**	**Short trek**
	Max days in park	20	7	3
High	15 Dec–31 Jan	$300	$50	$30
Medium	1–14 Dec	$200	$40	$20
	1–20 Feb			
Low	15–30 Nov	$100	$30	$20
	21 Feb–15 Mar			

The cost of permits depends on the activity and length of stay in the park, and whether it is high, low or medium season.

Permits are issued from Monday to Friday from 8am to 6pm, and on Saturday and Sunday from 9am to 1pm. The centre is closed on Christmas Day and New Year's Day.

At the park entrance the permit must be shown and passports checked (Horcones Valley side only – the first check on the Vacas Valley route is at Pampa de Leñas). Each trekker is issued with a refuse sack, which must be brought back out, full. Out-of-season permits are the same cost as high-season permits. Daily permits can be purchased at the Horcones ranger station for $US10.

TRAVEL AND CLIMBING INSURANCE

International travel agents can arrange both travel and climbing insurance, and at approximately $100 it is a worthwhile investment. These agents will not generally be alarmed at the height of the mountain, but will likely restrict cover to exclude technical climbing, such as vertical face work.

Anyone who has to be airlifted by helicopter out of base camp will have to pay for the privilege, irrespective of the unfortunate patient's condition.

PREPARATIONS

In Mendoza or Santiago, before and after the climb, shorts, T-shirts and light summer clothing will sufficient. This is the middle of summer, and even at night the temperature will be in the low 20s. The summer months in Mendoza may see an occasional downpour, but this is extremely rare.

For the walk in to base camp shorts and T-shirts will again be appropriate, but warmer clothing and waterproofs should be carried. Protection from the sun during the two-to-three-day walk should not be underestimated.

Crampons, double plastic boots and down jacket are essential

Summer clothing can be stored away at base camp. Whilst it will be warm in the middle of the day, temperatures in the morning and afternoon will dictate warmer clothing.

A number of items of non-standard gear are required on Aconcagua:
• down jacket
• double plastic boots
• crampons
• ice axe
• harness (possibly)
• -18°C sleeping bag
• sleeping mattress
• pee bottle

A down jacket is essential for the long cold evenings at base camp and above, and will probably be used at the top camp as a supplement to the -18°C sleeping bag at night.

Similarly double plastic boots are essential above base camp, as leather boots will freeze. There are varieties of insulated leather boots that will be adequate at base camp and the lower camps, providing they are taken into the tent at night and left in the sun in the morning to thaw. However, for the top camps there is no substitute for the double plastics, and virtually every climber on Aconcagua wears them. Some walk in from the road head in them, dispensing with the weight of trekking boots. The rangers now list double plastic boots and crampons as compulsory above the base camps.

During the ascent to the higher camps it gets much colder and windier. Climbers generally only bring the double plastics, keeping the inner boot on the foot during the night at top camp. Wind bloc fleeces are essential, and as soon as the sun sets the down jacket will be required.

For summit day you must be prepared to set off in the dark when the temperature will be at least -10°C, and the wind-chill factor will lower that significantly. The morning temperature may be so severe that the down jacket will be worn until dawn. As the day progresses the temperature will rise, so a layering system for all parts of the body should be automatic, including a balaclava and wool hat, several layers of gloves, and so on. Small lithium disposable hand warmers, slipped into the palm of the glove, can be a beneficial source of heat on a cold morning.

The ice axe, harness and crampons may only be required for summit day. Some guides will dispense with a harness because they can put together an adequate makeshift one from a length of rope. The pee bottle (with funnel for ladies) is required to obviate the need to exit the tent at the higher altitude.

The ground surface on the mountain is stony. In all the campsites the ground will be too hard for timber or steel tent pegs, so tents will be held down with boulders. Mattresses are a necessity.

Items of standard gear include:
- pair of walking poles
- category 4 sunglasses with nose and side shields (two pairs)
- walking boots
- day backpack (40 litres)
- large rucksack (80 litres)
- sun-hats
- bandanas
- gaiters to keep snow out of boots

The likelihood is that only the

Be prepared for heavy snow

Survival tip

A satchel that slips into the top of the rucksack can store valuables safely, including the camera. It can be used in both the city and around the camps, when a rucksack is awkward and hot.

Snow clearing at Plaza de Mulas

large rucksack will be taken above base camp. Daypacks are too small for carrying loads from camp to camp, and bringing the daypack for summit day alone may be seen as a luxury. Use the large rucksack on summit day. If you tend to have attachments to your final assault rucksack – for ice axe, crampons and walking poles – prepare it at base camp.

A mule will carry the gear into base camp. It will not stop at the intermediate camps in the valley approach, so mattress and sleeping bag will have to be carried in the daypack. A sturdy gear bag is recommended, as it will suffer considerable abuse on the back of a mule.

Rivers have to be crossed on the valley approaches. There are two bridges in the Horcones Valley and

one in the Vacas Valley where the river is deep, but you still have to cross shallower sections a number of times. Gore-Tex boots and the pair of walking poles will be invaluable. In the Vacas Valley you have to wade, jump or be carried across the river several times. A pair of plimsoles or trainers may be most worthwhile for these crossings, because the water is ice cold and the riverbed quite uneven.

The severe winds in the valleys whip up the dust. Bandanas or neckerchiefs are good protection against driving dust and sand. Sunglasses will be worn throughout the day, so should be comfortable. Those with effective nose and side shields are an absolute necessity, so it is strongly recommended to bring a spare pair.

51

The seasoned trekker will want to refine his gear to the bare essentials so that it is as light as possible. Here are a few tips:

- At base camp there will be ample time to wash clothes, and drying conditions will be ideal; even heavy woollen socks will dry in a few hours
- High on the mountain sweat is not an issue. Few will have the energy or inclination to brave the cold to change regularly
- If you have to buy crampons and ice axes check out the various weights. Some manufacturers, such as Camp and Cassin, produce lightweight gear
- Western airlines tend to have a lenient approach to excess baggage, but this is not the case in South America. At over $33 per excess kilo you could be faced with a hefty bill on the return journey

Survival tip

For those who write a diary, ballpoint pens are very susceptible to freezing at high altitude. Keep them warm. Fountain pens are less likely to freeze, but bring a pencil, just in case.

Wading through the Relinchos river

MEDICAL KIT

A few non-standard items should be included in the medical bag with your usual first-aid kit.

- Sun protection factor 25 (or higher) for up the mountain; factor 10 for the approach
- The wind will dry and chafe the lips, so cream protection and repair is necessary. Lip-healing ointment is a most sought-after product at the road head where climbers recover after their summit attempt
- Bowel-release and bowel-stop pills
- Facial wipes will prevent you from getting too dirty and smelly where water is scarce

The altitude has differing affects on people, and strangely seems to affect the young more than the mature. Headaches, feelings of nausea and sickness are common, and few will escape without some discomfort. Ibuprofen is regarded as most effective at relieving altitude headache, whilst nifedipine is the recommended treatment for pulmonary oedema.

There is a diversity of opinion on the use of Diamox (medical name acetazolamide). Originally prescribed for glaucoma, it has been found effective in alleviating altitude sickness. It generally comes in 250mg tablet form, and a typical dose is half a tablet twice each day.

Medical opinion is that the medication can do no harm. It has even been suggested that doubling or tripling the dose is better. Diamox does have side effects, such as tingling of the tips of the fingers and toes (which should not be misinterpreted as frostbite in the hallucinatory periods on summit day!). A secondary side effect is tenderness in the fingers and toes that can linger for a few weeks after medication has ceased. Diamox has also been known to cause severe allergic reactions, and those allergic to sulfa drugs should not take it.

Dexamethasone is a steroid that decreases brain and other swelling, reversing the effects of acute mountain sickness. It must be prescribed by a doctor who will be aware of the potential side effects. Dexamethasone can be combined with Diamox.

Diamox does increase dehydration and, on an arid mountain like Aconcagua, this is a significant issue. The consumption of copious amounts of liquid is vital for those at high altitude, and 4–5 litres per day should be regarded as a minimum. Very often simply the immediate drinking of a litre of water can dispel a headache or a nausea attack. Guides will recommend that the daily rate of 4–5 litres be increased by a litre for those taking Diamox.

Liquid intake can be divided between water, tea or coffee, juices, soups and so on, with less emphasis on tea and coffee, which can be diuretic. Of course, the more you drink the more you will need to urinate. This is not a problem during the day, but at night dressing up to go out in the cold is not recommended – hence the need for a dedicated pee bottle. The pee bottle should be at least 1.5 litres capacity (or use two 1-litre bottles), with a wide brim. Collapsible pee bottles are most useful. Those of similar size and shape to drink bottles are obviously not a good idea.

OTHER CONSIDERATIONS

Aconcagua is a difficult mountain and requires considerable preparation. A superior level of fitness is essential to success, and summit day requires stamina and endurance – pure, brute doggedness. Occasional spurts of training will obviously be inferior to long bouts in the hills, on the road or in the gym.

Feet do not break in double plastic boots: the boots break in the feet. Your feet should be accustomed to the rigidity of the boots, especially at the heels and ankles.

Fitting crampons, removing and refitting them should be second nature.

On summit day you may have to put them on in the dark, so you should be adept at strapping them tight.

There will be a small degree of ropework, so familiarity with knots and hooking up are important.

Getting ready for summit day should start before the expedition begins, and be reassessed at base camp. Have a checklist of clothing and gear. A simple deficiency that may not matter elsewhere could be the difference between summiting and failure. What will you eat? Don't rely on someone handing you a suitable package for the day, or being able to put something suitable together. Consider bringing a container of food from home that is non-perishable, can be eaten if frozen, and does not require excessive chewing.

These are perhaps the special requirements of Aconcagua. Spending two to three weeks in a tent, living out of a rucksack, caring for your feet, reading, eating and stumbling around by head torch are discomforts that can be learned.

ACCLIMATISATION

GETTING USED TO THIN AIR

Perhaps the most important element in a successful expedition on such a high mountain is acclimatisation. The longer you spend either at base camp and the lower camps, or at other high elevations, the better you will be at high altitude.

Acclimatising on another mountain, such as Vallecitos or El Plomo, can be particularly valuable, but will involve additional organisation, time and expense. Trekking in and around the provincial park is an easy alternative. Professional guiding companies, recognising the great advantage of pre-acclimatisation, offer packages of two peaks in the Andes, such as Vallecitos–Aconcagua or El Plomo–Aconcagua.

As soon as you get off the bus at Los Penitentes or Puente del Inca the thin air becomes apparent. Breathlessness follows even minor degrees of physical effort, and it takes time to get accustomed to this. A slow build-up is recommended. Early exertions can lead to nausea and sickness. However, there is equally little point in being too careful, in taking things too easy. You must gauge how your own body is affected, and if exertions are showing no ill effects then further exertion should be made. Leaving base camp to rise steeply, without having experienced tough physical

Stretching the legs at Los Penitentes

exertion at altitude, will not bode well for a successful climb.

The climbers' maxim of 'walking high, sleeping low' is tried and trusted. After arrival and a rest at the next camp the climber should proceed further up the mountain to gain higher altitude before retiring for the night. The universal recommendation is to restrict climbs to 1000m per day, and to rest for a day after every 3000m, but these levels are appropriate for experienced climbers. Restricting the daily elevation change to 600m should be the target.

Always sleep with the head raised slightly. On sloping ground the tent should be orientated so that the climbers' heads are at the highest elevation.

RECOGNISING ALTITUDE SICKNESS

The Associatión Argentina de Guías Profesionales de Montaña (AAGPM) publishes a useful leaflet under the auspices of the Mendoza government. This awards points for medical/physical conditions and recommends appropriate treatment.

The onset of pulmonary oedema will be preceded by nausea and vomiting. A severe headache may be the precursor to cerebral oedema. However, most climbers will feel nausea, and few will escape without a headache, so that when these symptoms materialise there should be no sense of panic. For most the consumption of a litre of water and rest will cure the ailment. Where the symptoms continue or worsen a measurement of saturated oxygen will determine if more effective action is necessary. This will generally entail descending. Recovery from a cerebral ailment will be faster than recovery from a pulmonary ailment.

The words 'hypoxia' or 'anoxia' may often be heard in relation to altitude ailments. Hypoxia is a

Symptoms
- Headache, nausea, loss of appetite and dizziness: 1 point
- Vomiting and headaches that are resistant to aspirin/paracetamol: 2 points
- Shortness of breath at rest, abnormal fatigue and a low urine volume: 3 points

Treatment
- Up to 3 points: Aspirin/paracetamol is recommended, with plenty of water
- 3–6 points: It is recommended that ascending ceases, that the climber rests, drinks and takes aspirin/paracetamol, again with copious amounts of water
- Above 6 points: The climber is advised to descend

BREAKFAST AT LOS PENITENTES

When the early bustle of climbers at the hotel had subsided there were two British climbers remaining. Both had been forced to abandon their climb prematurely.

Alan from Leeds, who was in his forties and had been to an altitude of 3600m before coming to Aconcagua, had come down from Camp Canada suffering from pulmonary oedema. His breakfast companion, Richard from Reading, was a little younger. He had been brought down from Nido de Condores with cerebral oedema. They both described their experiences.

Alan had no difficulty on his initial visit to Camp Canada. It was when the team moved there to sleep that he found breathing difficult. He was sick and had chronic diarrhoea. When he arrived down at Plaza de Mulas the doctor recorded his saturated oxygen at only 63 per cent and ordered him airlifted out immediately. He recounted how the pilot had great difficulty with the helicopter in the wind, trying to avoid hitting the sides of the valley. Alan had had a bad night in Los Penitentes and was waiting for transport down to Mendoza.

Richard, on the other hand, had made a complete recovery, had eaten dinner the night before and was tucking into a hearty breakfast. His transport out from Plaza de Mulas was by mule.

deficiency of oxygen in arterial blood and/or in the tissues, and oedema is one form of hypoxia.

SATURATED OXYGEN

As part of its services in policing the Aconcagua Provincial Park the local government in Mendoza sponsors medical tents at Plaza de Mulas and Plaza Argentina where climbers are invited to be checked before they ascend.

The most important aspect of this check is saturated oxygen level, which is normally done with a small pulse oximeter. The device is placed over the index finger. It transmits red and infrared light through the finger and detects fluctuating signals caused by blood flow. The ratio of the fluctuation of the light signals is used to calculate the blood oxygen saturation ($\%SPO_2$).

Haemoglobin molecules in the blood carry oxygen. For a healthy person at rest at sea level the percentage of haemoglobin molecules that carry oxygen could, theoretically, be as high as 100 per cent but, practically, a little less than this. As one ascends it is natural for some of the molecules not to carry oxygen. However, the higher the number that do carry oxygen the better.

The doctor checks saturated oxygen at Plaza Argentina

Target saturated oxygen levels	
Altitude (m)	Target %SPO^2
Zero	97
1500	93
2000	92
4000	88
5000	83
6000	77

At the base camps, where the altitude is approximately 4250m, a SPO^2 in the upper 80s is desirable, and some will register over 90. A count under 80 will generally be accompanied by advice to stay at base camp, relax and drink. A count of less than 70 may come with a recommendation to descend.

GUIDES AND MULES

GUIDES AND THEIR NECESSITY

With only the simple word 'Aconcagua' search engines on the Internet will display countless companies and individuals providing guided tours up the mountain. There is the choice of joining a group in one's own country, joining a group in Mendoza organised by local Argentineans, or going solo.

There is no requirement to hire a guide, and a significant number of climbers and trekkers opt to travel unaccompanied. Mules can be hired on an individual basis at the road head, or in advance through the mule companies. At Confluencia, Plaza de

Mulas and Plaza Argentina there are restaurants (fairly limited and basic). At Plaza de Mulas there is even a hotel, with full shower, toilet and restaurant facilities, and an international telephone link. However, there are no shops on the mountain, so all provisions for the higher camps must be carried.

There are great advantages in hiring a local guide, or joining a locally organised group. The guides know the mountain, speak the language, and most important, can read the weather. When mini crises arise – as they often do – a local guide's help can be invaluable. The mountain is his

An expedition team at the Horcones trail head

Survival tip

A word of warning: if it is proposed to hire a guide then choose carefully. A bad guide may be worse than no guide.

livelihood, guiding his profession. He will have summited many times, and altitude will have little effect on him. The various guides know each another, so that when one runs out of an essential commodity he knows he can get help.

Local guides will know the medical doctor on duty, and how to raise him in an emergency. Those who ascend unguided should be reasonably confident that altitude will not cause problems for them. Guides will help unguided travellers in an emergency, but with a degree of reluctance. Your guide will discourage you from inviting unguided travellers to accompany the trek, no matter how companionable they are.

The tour operators on the mountain provide toilet facilities for their clients. This is a much more convenient service than collecting your own waste and carrying it in your refuse sack, or trying to purchase latrine facilities at the base camp.

CHOOSING A GUIDE

A licensed high mountain guide in Argentina must undergo two periods of training, each lasting 20 weeks,

High-mountain guides Pablo Reguera and Mauricio Fernández

Important

- Transfers, hospitalization and medications' expenses outside the park are not included in our permit.
- The military regiment of Puente de Inca has   authorized to transport gear inside /outside the park.
- It is not permitted to camp in Inferior Plaza de Mulas (Military's camp)
- Trekkers are not permitted to camp in Plaza Francia.
- Every climber must hire a private restroom service in Plaza de Mulas base camp or Plaza Argentina (it is included in case your contract mules).
- For Aconcagua ascension is obligatory the use of crampers and double boots.
- Youngers than 21 years old, ask for conditions.

Sr. Andinista

- Los gastos de traslado, hospitalización y medicamentos fuera del parque no están incluidos en su permiso.
- El regimiento militar de Puente de Inca esta autorizado a transportar cargas. Está prohibido acampar en Plaza de Mulas (campamento militar).
      acampar en Plaza

Official notice at the permit office

one during the summer and the other during the winter. These guides will have a comprehensive medical kit, including stethoscope, syringes and bandages.

At the beginning of the 2003/2004 season the Mendoza government expected up to 65 professional guides to register, of which 25 would be qualified as high mountain guides (above 4500m). Obviously, there are not enough qualified guides to serve the high number of climbers.

The three largest operators have permanent compounds at the main campsites. When you arrive with the guide the tents are already in place, inside an enclosure including the mess tent. Others (non-guided) may have to clear stones and pitch wherever there is space available.

With guides and permanent compounds the three premier operators can take a party up one route and return via a different one. They will also tailor their service to the traveller's requirements. One popular service is to arrange pick-up from the airport, hotel in Mendoza, transportation to and from the mountain, and a mule service (but no mountain guide).

In selecting a guide the following obvious questions should be asked:

- Number of days allowed to summit? Any spare days? This is most important. Some guides have little motivation to take climbers to the summit. They have the attitude that the climber may accept that he/she was not capable/ ready, when in fact the climber was given inadequate time by the guide to acclimatise
- Guide/trekker ratio? A ratio of one guide for every three trekkers should be regarded as a minimum, especially for summit day. There must be adequate guides to bring down people who cannot go on
- Are the guides licensed?
- How many times has the guide(s) summited?
- What medical equipment will the guide have – Diamox, saturated oxygen monitor, bowel-control tablets, syringes, and so on?
- Will the guide have a radio to raise base camp?
- What food will be provided – normally, and on summit day?
- Hotel accommodation in Mendoza – single, double, quality?
- Tents – how many to a tent, size of tent?
- Cost implications of any special arrangements (for instance, up one route, return via a different route, visit Christ the Redeemer Statue or Plaza Francia for acclimatisation)?

Some operators, advertising on the Internet, offer a package that takes 15 days. This is much too optimistic for those who have no acclimatisation. Inevitably the summit attempt will fail, or the operator may claim an extra premium if the expedition time is extended.

TYPICAL ITINERARY FOR THE VACAS VALLEY ROUTE

Day	1	Arrive Mendoza
Day	2	Obtain permit and travel to Puente del Inca
Day	3	Start trek: Punta de Vacas to Pampa de Leñas
Day	4	Pampa de Leñas to Casa Piedra
Day	5	Casa Piedra to Plaza Argentina
Day	6	Rest day
Day	7	Visit camp 1
Day	8	Rest day
Day	9	Move to camp 1
Day	10	Visit camp 2
Day	11	Rest day
Day	12	Move to camp 2
Day	13	Rest day
Day	14	Move to camp 3
Day	15	Summit day
Day	16	Spare day
Day	17	Descend to base camp
Day	18	Base camp to intermediate camp
Day	19	Intermediate camp to road head
Day	20	Transport to Santiago or Mendoza
Day	21	Flight home

The duration should be regarded as a minimum for those who are not acclimatised. An extra day at Puente del Inca to go to the statue of Christ the Redeemer, and another around day 10, will assist with acclimatisation.

WITHOUT A GUIDE

Well-prepared seasoned travellers may want to climb the mountain without a guide – some even without a mule – and there is no restriction on them so doing. Travelling alone can have many benefits – it reduces costs significantly, you eat what and when you want, and are not hampered by the inability or pace of fellow travellers.

There is a question about a guide on the application form at the permit office, and this can be ignored. There will be no cross-examination about your skill or abilities. At the campsites with rangers on duty you will have to present your permit, possibly also your passport.

On the road and in the mountain parks there are no great dangers, no history of highwaymen, and the locals are usually very friendly. Language will be a barrier, but not an insurmountable one.

It is most important to make a detailed checklist of essential items for the trek. On the mountain cooked food can be purchased at the base camps, but otherwise there will be no means of acquiring foodstuffs or fuel except through barter with others.

THE ARRIEROS

The men who handle the mules on Aconcagua are known as arrieros. Some work for the big mule operators, but most are freelance agents hired on a weekly basis. Tremendously loyal to each other and their trade, they are all from the western plains of Argentina, where they spend the winters herding cattle.

Some trekkers will consider them cruel to the mules. However, in the author's experience they are a hard-working group of men with a wonderful sense of humour. Mules are stubborn animals that have to be continually controlled, and cannot be coaxed into action. A mule in the mountains holds the same value as a horse, and so is relatively valuable. Whereas a horse has to be fed in these arid lands, a mule will generally fend for itself, eating almost anything. There is a shortage of donkeys in Argentina, so mules – horse/donkey crosses – are becoming scarce.

The arrieros carry their *mate* in a satchel strewn across the mule. The *yerba mate* will be on one side, possibly with a separate pouch for sugar, and the gourd and bombilla on the other side. The arrieros' diet is meat, and plenty of it, cooked on an open fire, eaten, fat and all, with a large sharp knife.

The arrieros are a hardworking people

Arrieros return down the Horcones Valley after a long day

MATE

Drinking mate

Mate is South American tea. Made simply from grass and hot water it is drunk from a small vessel, or gourd, through a metal filter, or bombilla. The grass, or *yerba mate*, is grown in northern Argentina, southern Paraguay and Bolivia. Packed in 1kg bags it contains natural minerals and vitamins.

The custom of taking *mate* is popular in all of Argentina, southern Brazil, Peru and Paraguay, and is a national obsession in Bolivia. Very little is consumed in Chile.

When *mate* is taken one person will be in control. He/she will prepare the initial mixture, taste it and pass it around. The gourd will always be passed back to the controller; passing it directly to someone else is impolite. The taste is very bitter, but many add sugar to reduce this. A gourd filling will last from 10–30 water toppings. The advent of hot water flasks has made taking *mate* more convenient.

65

Mule station at Plaza de Mulas

HIRING MULES

Mules can be hired at the road head or at the base camps. It is generally the custom to contract for a round trip from the road head to base camp and back, and prices will vary considerably.

A mule should take no more than 60kg, 30kg on each side, and the mule companies may require special rates for loads that do not fit this arrangement. The arrieros jealously reserve the right to decide how loads are distributed and secured. A rate of between $120 and $150 will be sought for the first mule, and half of this for the next two mules. One arriero can drive no more than three mules, so the cost of the fourth mule may revert to the higher price, the fifth and sixth the lower price, and so on, but these rules are not always adhered to. The trekker will be unaware of the other arrangements the mule company is making, so that where he has paid for, say, two mules, his shipment may be part of an enormous mule train.

PART II

MENDOZA TO PUENTE DEL INCA

Mendoza

Mendoza is a bustling, relatively modern city of over 1 million inhabitants. Founded in the mid 16th century as a province of Santiago in Chile (and named after the then Captain General of Chile), Mendoza was virtually destroyed by the worst earthquake in South American history in 1861. The city was quickly rebuilt, with wide, tree-lined streets, a central plaza and four satellite plazas (named after the countries that helped in the rebuilding).

The French planner laid the modern city out on a grid pattern. Each street has a grass margin, with trees separating the footpath from the road. In this margin there is a deep trench that conveys water, coming down from the Andes, to irrigate the trees.

Maps of the city are available at every hotel reception. Essentially it is laid out on an (almost) north–south axis. The main artery, from the airport south through the city and out towards Chile/Aconcagua/Tupungato is Ave San Martin, commonly called the Alameda. Going west from the Alameda lies the main city centre, then Parque San Martin which rises up to the Andes.

From the city centre the snow-capped Andes are clearly visible (though not Aconcagua, which is blocked from view by a range of intermediate mountains). The Andes mountains are the second most important attraction of Mendoza for visitors, but only a small proportion come for Aconcagua.

The water from the Andes is fundamental to the economy and survival of Mendoza. The main river, Rio Mendoza, is dammed at Potrerillos, where much of the solids settle out. From here it is controlled to irrigate the vineyards, the agricultural lands, city trees and parks. Drinking water is taken from the Rio Blanco below Vallecitos and piped separately to the city. White-water rafting (and kayaking) is growing in popularity year by

Mendoza is the centre of winemaking in Argentina, and the Mendocinos have been making wine since the foundation of the city. Over 70 per cent of Argentina's wines are produced in Mendoza province, and the majority of the many visitors each year come on wine trips, visiting bodegas in and around Mendoza.

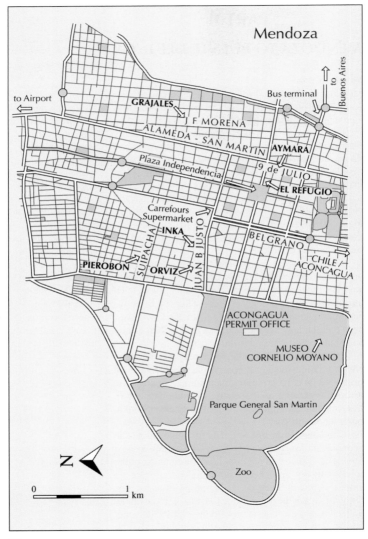

year, and the fast-flowing river above Potrerillos is ideal for this activity.

White-water rafting on the Rio Mendoza

For the mountaineer the city has all the necessary facilities. Some of the best gear shops in the world are here, and the costs are low. Hiring gear is also available. Supermarkets within the city and on the outskirts sell food suitable for camping. Internet cafés abound. Post offices (*correos*) and telephone establishments (*locotorrios*) are alternative, economic communications outlets.

Survival tip

From 2pm to 5pm is siesta time in Mendoza, when many small businesses close.

Buying provisions

The supermarkets of Mendoza are excellent sources of food for the mountain, but not all stock the specialist items that climbers seek. There are two Carrefours, for instance, one in the centre of the city on Belgrano.

The amount of provisions for a two-week trek will differ from individual to individual. Some will want a varied diet, whilst others will bring a limited number of tried and trusted foodstuffs. The experienced will adopt the same strategy for food as for clothes: take the bare essentials, and avoid bringing items that *might* be useful – they have to be carried. However, fluids are probably more important than solids, and six extra soups weigh much less than a kilo of vegetables.

The most popular form of cooking is liquid paraffin via a pressurised bottle. This commodity is cheap and transferable, and is likely to be one of the heaviest loads to be carried. Standard gas canisters are also readily available.

Fruit for sale by the roadside

The following suggestions may be helpful:

- The water that is available on the mountain comes from melted snow and ice, and contains no minerals or nutrients. Supplements, in the form of flavoured sachets, provide these ingredients and are widely available

- Powdered food – such as egg, semolina, milk and potato – are a good and palatable form of food that is easily prepared. Powdered egg is not easy to source. Tea bags, coffee, sugar, soup and the like are freely available. Tea or flavoured herbal mixes may be less harsh on the stomach than coffee, particularly taken in large quantities. Bags of muesli and breakfast cereals, including porridge, are popular. Many shops sell an array of nuts that can be added to muesli

- Argentinean fruit and vegetables are wonderful. Oranges and grapefruits are relatively large, but not easily damaged, and provide a welcome juice source. The local tomatoes are particularly large and succulent. A dish of tomatoes and onions, sprinkled with olive oil and a herb-garlic pepper, takes little time to prepare. Fruit and vegetables, however, must be protected from frost. Canned forms are not as nourishing or appetising, are heavier, but last longer

- Argentina and Chile produce quality beef and lamb. Getting meat up to base camp requires an insulated cooler; there is no traffic in live fowl or animals. Tinned meat is the alternative (generally not available in supermarkets, but in the smaller shops). Specialised boil-in-the-bag meals are not easy to find, and ready-meals are of little use without a microwave. Salami and cheese are great for lunch, and can last the duration of an expedition if protected

A benzene stove is the most popular form of cooking

Casa de Fader where Fernando Fader's paintings are housed

Typical paintings of Fernando Fader, Mendoza's renowned artist

The road to Puente del Inca

There are three roads out of Mendoza going south towards Chile, Aconcagua and Tupungato. The fastest is the motorway (*autopista*). The most interesting – but also the slowest – is the old route through the vineyards, via the suburb of Lujan. Of further interest along this route is the house of Fernando Fader, the great Mendocino artist whose impressionist style made him world famous.

The long-distance public buses that travel between Santiago and Mendoza are of excellent quality and relatively inexpensive. The buses from Mendoza stop at Uspallata, an interesting town at an elevation of 1850m. The town was formerly a centre for iron-ore smelting, manufacturing cannon-balls for the army that swept down into Chile to defeat the Spanish in 1818. In recent times the area became famous as the location for the making of the film *Seven Years in Tibet*.

On the approach to Uspallata there is a busy restaurant on the right-hand side, 2km from the village centre. This is Estancia Elias, the best place to eat between Mendoza and Aconcagua. Their *parilla* is particularly good.

Buses do not stop, unless prearranged, at Los Penitentes, Punta de Vacas or Puente del Inca, but it is possible to embark and disembark at Las Cuevas. The cost of a bus ride from the border to either Mendoza or Santiago should be no more than a few dollars. The payment will, almost certainly, go directly into the pockets of the driver and courier, so a little bargaining may be required.

Mendoza-to-Santiago disused railway

The Mendoza-to-Santiago railway is a most interesting feature of the landscape that runs parallel to the road all the way from city to city. It was built between 1890 and 1920, and its scale is an indication of the wealth of the region during that period. There are numerous tunnels and bridges. All the sleepers on the Argentinean side are timber, but the Chileans opted for steel sleepers in the mountains.

Damaged structure on the Mendoza-to-Santiago railway

The ski resort of Los Penitentes with Tolosa mountain in the background

When it opened in the 1920s it carried both goods and passengers along the 350km journey. Subject to regular rockslides and subsidence the railway required costly maintenance. At Las Cuevas, for instance, the enormous boulders on the line that rolled down in an avalanche are testament to this. Eventually the line that took so much effort to construct was allowed to fall into disrepair, and was closed permanently in the 1980s.

Nowadays the drone of juggernauts and buses has replaced the less intrusive sound of steam.

◀ Los Penitentes

Los Penitentes is the most popular stop for climbers. It is a ski resort with a cable car and a number of hotels. During the summer only one or two establishments are open.

Southeast of Los Penitentes lies Punta de Vacas. This is essentially an army base that caters for long-distance trucks. It has no shop or hotel. If you walk far enough towards Punta de Vacas, at a bend in the road, there is a clear view of Tupungato.

Los Penitentes is at an elevation of 2580m, so altitude effects will begin here for those who are not acclimatised. A good policy is to walk around to start the process.

◀ Puente del Inca

Puente del Inca is a better, less expensive, place to stay than Los Penitentes. It is closer to the Horcones road

It would be most unfortunate for the traveller to come →

head and is full of life. By contrast, the juggernauts do not even change gear when going through Los Penitentes.

The village takes its name from the natural bridge over the River Las Cuevas, only 50m from the main road. The bridge may be accessed on foot via a wide lane that has souvenir stalls on either side. The banks of the river are coloured a bright orange by the sulphur from the hot springs. Notices by the bridge display how it was formed – an ice bridge over the river was covered by an avalanche of boulders that were then cemented together by sulphur from the springs. The ice melted, and the 'bridge' remained.

A hotel was built in 1917, specifically for the clients to take the hot springs, with a tunnel connecting the hotel to the baths under the bridge. The hotel thrived until 1965 when an enormous avalanche destroyed it. The baths, though now disused, can still provide a refreshing hot shower.

Of the places to stay in Puente del Inca the army hostel is worth considering. Over the entrance door to the army barracks (Ejercito Argentina) is a sign welcoming all mountaineers. The dedicated visitors' hostel, suitable for

← to Aconcagua and not experience Puente del Inca. The natural wonder of the bridge and its thermal waters should not be missed.

The natural bridge over the Las Cuevas river at Puente del Inca

75

The Andinista graveyard

both sexes, can accommodate 76 visitors in bunk-bed-ded rooms with separate bathrooms. Though the bedrooms are rather basic, the ground-floor reception rooms are spacious and comfortable, and the food is good. This is the cheapest accommodation for Aconcagua.

Between Puente del Inca and Los Penitentes is the Andinistas graveyard, where many of those who have died on Aconcagua are buried. This is a relatively short walk from Los Penitentes.

ACONCAGUA ROUTES

The Normal Route

At the start of the route there is a gravel car park near a ranger station, with a helicopter permanently parked nearby. This is used to take medical and emergency supplies to the various base camps, and to airlift sick or injured climbers out. It is in constant use, generally landing at both base camps at least once every day. Since its introduction in the 1999/2000 season the number of fatalities on the mountain annually has dropped from seven to ten to one to two.

The ruta Normal begins about 5km west of Puente del Inca, or 10km from Los Penitentes.

The ranger will check the permits and issue refuse sacks. The non-return of a refuse sack carries a fine of up to $US100. Guides will always take charge of their client's refuse sack.

There is a dirt track road in for a few kilometres, but its use for vehicles is discouraged except in emergencies. About 2.5km in is the lagoon, where undoubtedly more photographs will be taken. The road is stony and flat as

The start of the Normal route at the Horcones road head

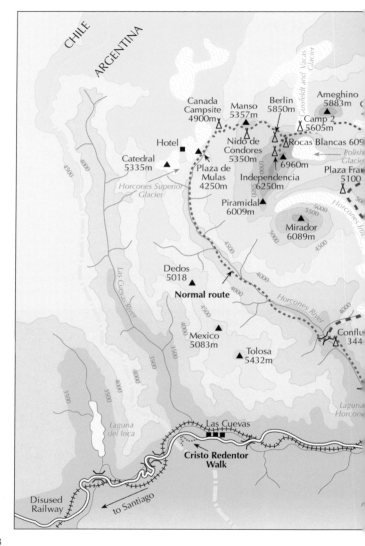

CHILE

ARGENTINA

Canada
Campsite
4900m

Manso
5357m

Berlin
5850m

Gussfeldt and Vacas
Glacier

Ameghino
5883m

Camp 2
5605m

Hotel

Nido de
Condores
5350m

Rocas Blancas 609

Catedral
5335m

Plaza de
Mulas
4250m

Independencia
6250m

6960m

*Polish
Glacie*

Plaza Fra
5100

*Horcones Superior
Glacier*

Piramidal
6009m

Horcones Infe

Mirador
6089m

Dedos
5018

Normal route

Horcones River

Mexico
5083m

Tolosa
5432m

Las Cuevas River

Conflu
344

*Laguna
Horcone*

*Laguna
del Inca*

Las Cuevas

**Cristo Redentor
Walk**

Disused
Railway

to Santiago

78

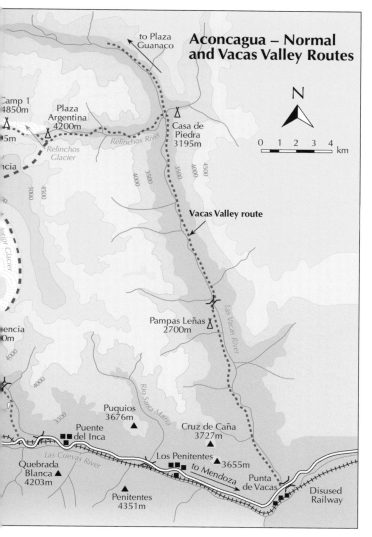

Aconcagua – Normal and Vacas Valley Routes

to Plaza Guanaco

Camp 1 4850m

Plaza Argentina 4200m

Relinchos Glacier

Relinchos River

Casa de Piedra 3195m

Vacas Valley route

N

0 1 2 3 4 km

Pampas Leñas 2700m

Las Vacas River

encia 0m

Puquios 3676m

Cruz de Caña 3727m

Rio Santa Maria

Puente del Inca

Las Cuevas River

Los Penitentes 3655m

to Mendoza

Punta de Vacas

Disused Railway

Quebrada Blanca 4203m

Penitentes 4351m

far as the first footbridge – a gentle introduction to the ruta Normal. This steel suspension bridge was erected some years ago over the raging torrent below. After the footbridge the path initially follows the river on its eastern bank, then leaves the river to rise steeply through a grey limestone boulder field before easing out to a gentle gradient on the approach to Confluencia.

For these first two days of the journey to base camp you will have to carry everything you need during the day and for the night in Confluencia: sleeping bag, mattress and warm clothing will be essential. The mules will have

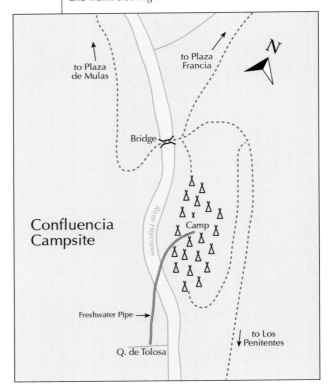

The Confluencia camp viewed from higher up the trail

gone ahead direct to Plaza de Mulas with the main loads. Confluencia will be reached in about three hours. It is a sheltered campsite, set in a valley, with the river alongside. Some will rest here for a day; some will trek up to Plaza Francia and return. Those on their way out may only pause to take on water. There is fresh water, piped from a clear source to the southwest (where the former *Confluencia* was located).

From the road head to Confluencia the altitude will have increased from 2580m to 3440m. It will be hot during the day at Confluencia, as high as 27°C, falling when the sun goes down to perhaps 6°C at night.

Confluencia will probably provide the trekker's first experience of the use of the mountain's toilet facilities. The larger trek operators will have enclosed toilet cubicles – a heavy plastic covering around a metal frame, with a hole in the ground over a sunken barrel. The operators now guard their toilets, and generally keep them locked. At the end of the season they have to remove the sunken barrel. Those who have not come with a trek →

81

← operator must find alternative places. The ranger on duty will be vigilant at Confluencia, since this is the first campsite. Trekkers are required to take away their waste in their refuse sacks.

The park authorities propose, in the near future, to construct the mountain's first communal toilet facilities at Confluencia, and to follow this with similar facilities at the base camps.

From Confluencia to **Plaza de Mulas** takes six to eight hours. Initially the path runs over the river flood plain, a flat walk over gravel. You will have to cross the river three times, and if the river is full the water will cover your boots. Some will take off their boots and wade through the ice-cold water, others will run and jump, and the more practical will keep their boots on, using their walking poles to limit the damage, and wringing their socks out to dry at midday.

Near to base camp the trail becomes dramatically steeper. Plaza de Mulas is at an elevation of 4250m, and the last few kilometres account for most of the rise.

At the height of the season expect to find upwards of 150 tents and 50 mess tents, so that the population could be several hundred people. It is a relatively sheltered campsite, with fresh water running along its northeastern side, near the exit route up the mountain.

Crossing the Horcones river at a shallow point

High costs for ablution facilities at Plaza de Mulas

▶ There are a number of places to eat and drink at base camp, with burgers, steak sandwiches and beer very popular. Hygiene is not a strong point in these makeshift cafés, however, and there have been incidences of diarrhoea.

Upon arrival at base camp it is advisable to get an early indication of your saturated oxygen level. The service is free and encouraged, and the doctor's tent is in the middle of the camp. Virtually everyone takes at least one day's rest at Plaza de Mulas, some two days or more, depending on the saturated oxygen count.

Survival tip: The telephones at Hotel Plaza de Mulas take only Argentinean peso coins.

A short walk to the west from base camp is the **Hotel Plaza de Mulas**, where you can telephone the outside world, have a meal, take a shower. En route to the hotel you will encounter your first field of penitentes. The walk over to the hotel takes 20 minutes, over undulating ground: an energy-sapping experience for the unacclimatised newcomer. At the hotel there is great demand for the two telephones in the front hall. Most tour operators have satellite mobile phones for client use, but charges are considerably more expensive than the hotel's landline. There are Internet facilities at Plaza de Mulas (also quite expensive).

Above Plaza de Mulas there are three intermediate camps before the summit:

- **Camp Canada** (4900m)
- **Nido de Condores** (5350m), and finally
- **Berlin** (5850m)

The camps at Canada and Nido de Condores are ill-defined, with tents pitched in no particular pattern. At Canada the campsite is south of the route up the mountain, and at Nido the route is through the campsite. At Berlin the camp is on a shoulder of the mountain, and the tents are tightly grouped around a number of wooden huts.

Nido de Condores was elevated in 2002 to somewhat the same status as the base camps, and now has a park ranger resident. This reflects the numbers who camp there. Some may bypass Camp Canada, and some may make their summit bid direct from Nido, but few bypass Nido.

The ranger here has significant authority. He is required to check on the condition of climbers, and may call to tents. He can order climbers to descend if he suspects a poor medical or physical condition, or if he

The route out of Plaza de Mulas towards Camp Canada

discovers that a climber does not have the proper gear for this altitude.

The route between Camp Canada and Nido de Condores

None of the upper camps have fresh water, so snow must be gathered for melting. Berlin can be particularly cramped. Behind most boulders there are the inevitable excrement deposits, so finding fresh, clean snow may require a climb.

Whereas the trail into Plaza de Mulas is generally relatively flat (except for the last few kilometres) it changes significantly above the base camp. Out over the field of *penitentes* from Plaza de Mulas the route is quite steep and only eases upon reaching **Camp Canada**. It is a three-hour trek up to Canada and a further three hours to Nido. The Berlin camp is a four-hour trek above Nido.

As the altitude increases the night-time temperature and wind-chill become more significant. At base camp there can be a considerable degree of movement around the camp at night. There will be discussions and the occasional singsong. At the upper camps the cold will drive all into their sleeping bags as soon as the sun sets, and few will venture out until the sun shines on the tent again in the morning.

A well-worn path through penitentes on the Normal route

Up to **Nido de Condores** the emphasis will be on steady trekking, acclimatisation, taking things easy, regular resting, carrying a load up to return and sleep at a lower camp. After Nido that pattern changes. Upon reaching **Berlin** the focus is on the summit. Spending a rest day at an altitude of 5850m is not to be recommended. The air is thin, it is difficult to sleep, appetites are poor and the weather can be treacherous. The plan is to make ready at Berlin and set off early the next morning for the summit (see page 93).

In the late afternoon at Berlin climbers will be returning from their summit attempt. Those who have made it will be in high spirits and may continue their celebrations into the night, much to the annoyance of those who are trying to gain a degree of peaceful repose (sleep might be too much to hope for) before their early morning venture. There will be drama too as anxious eyes scan the skyline at dusk for comrades who are on their way down. There will be the occasional scramble from the camp to help exhausted climbers make it back.

The sunsets at Berlin can be spectacular, and well worth staying up for. As every mountain climber knows, the sky at night over such places can be so clear, the stars so vivid.

The Vacas Valley Route

Activity at the road head here is much quieter than further west at the start of the Normal route. There is no ranger, no helicopter, and no mule station. A ruined stone hut is the only distinguishing landmark.

Steeper and more rugged than the Normal route, the trail rises and falls with the river, winding over steep scree. There is good shelter from the sun and wind, however. You will be aware immediately of the solitude, only interrupted by scurrying lizards and singing birds.

The initial journey ends after four to five hours at **Pampa de Leñas**, at an elevation of 2700m, so the height gained on the first day is very small. There will only be a few tents at this campsite, where the ranger and his family live. The area is nestled under high cliffs, sheltered and peaceful, with running water in the river alongside.

The Vacas Valley route starts at Punta de Vacas, 7km east of Los Penitentes.

AN ENCOUNTER AT PAMPA DE LEÑAS

Two Londoners were resting at Pampa de Leñas, en route from Plaza Argentina to Punta de Vacas. They were originally three, but one had to be airlifted out due to altitude sickness. The two had reached Camp 2 and were preparing for a summit attempt. It was extremely cold in the early morning, the temperature at -15°C. One of them had removed his gloves in order to put on and tie his boots. When he put the gloves back on he could not get circulation back into all his fingers. Nevertheless he started the climb. After an hour he stopped and discussed his problem with the guide. Vain attempts were made to warm his hands, but it was not possible to get the blood in his thumbs to circulate. Eventually he returned to camp, and his comrade proceeded to the summit. Warm water failed to relieve the problem. At base camp the doctor had bandaged the thumbs, but was doubtful that they could be saved. They were now turning black.

The friends further related how they had been in the company of a Korean on the inward journey from Punta de Vacas. At Pampa de Leñas the Korean had decided to flex his muscles by climbing the cliff above the camp. He had fallen and was seriously injured. They were now informed that he had died on the way to hospital.

<PARQUE PROVINCIAL ACONCAGUA

- Quebrada del Rio Vacas -

▲ PAMPA DE LEÑAS — 2.800 m.s.n.m. — a 5 Hs.
▲ CASA DE PIEDRA — 3.200 m.s.n.m. — a 11 Hs.
▲ PLAZA ARGENTINA — 4.200 m.s.n.m. — a 18 Hs.>

The sign at the Vacas Valley roadhead

The trail on the second day, to **Casa de Piedra**, is very similar, once again with very little elevation achieved. On the journey you will cross a footbridge 1km north of Pampa de Leñas and later see cattle grazing on the river's edge.

On arrival at Casa de Piedra there is a wonderful view of Aconcagua from the Polish Glacier side. As you enter the campsite clearing Cerro Ameghino initially comes into view, followed later by the awesome bulk of Aconcagua.

Casa de Piedra (3195m) is a disjointed campsite alongside the river. There is a rough stone structure – from which the site gets its name – built into an enormous isolated rock on the eastern bank. The arrieros will camp in and around this. Some climbers will choose to cross the river immediately and camp, so that boots and socks can be dried out by morning. Other will have arranged for mule transport over the river in the morning, and will camp on the eastern bank. The river here has many tributaries, so there are multiple crossing points.

The trail from Casa de Piedra up the **Relinchos Valley** is tough. There are many climbs around the steep valley

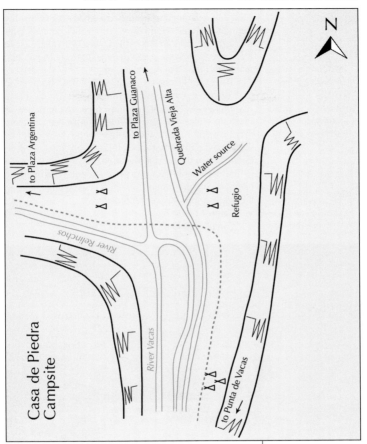

to Plaza Argentina

to Plaza Guanaco

Quebrada Vieja Alta

Water source

Refugio

River Relinchos

River Vacas

Casa de Piedra Campsite

to Punta de Vacas

sides, and a few river crossings. One crossing must be made approximately a third of the way up, where the river is deep and fast flowing. The water is ice-cold and the riverbed stony.

Plaza Argentina is at roughly the same elevation as Plaza de Mulas (4200m). It is five to six hours' walk from

The Casa de Piedra to Plaza Argentina stretch is where you are most likely to see guanacos (a few dead ones, at least).

Casa de Piedra up through the Relinchos river valley. The Relinchos Glacier runs down this valley and dictates much of the trail. Similar to the Lower Horcones Glacier it is covered in scree, eventually giving way to flat land that leads into Plaza Argentina. ◄

The camp lies on an undulating glacial moraine, so that many of the tents are hidden from view. Plaza Argentina has the same facilities, on a smaller scale, as Plaza de Mulas. Here, at the height of the season, there may be up to 50 tents and 15 mess tents. The doctor and the ranger will be here, but there is no hotel, and no phone link to the outside world.

Above Plaza Argentina there are three intermediate camps before the summit (attempts at assigning names to the lower camps have so far failed):

The footbridge over the Vacas river outside Pampa de Leñas

- **Camp 1** (4850m)
- **Camp 2** (5605m), and finally

- **Rocas Blancas** (6095m)

  The climb from base camp to **Camp 1** is a gruelling five hours through fields of *penitentes*, and over a glacier with rough scree deposits. Often you have the choice of scrambling over loose gravelly moraine or negotiating a way through the *penitentes*. The eventual approach in to Camp 1 is a left-hand turn over deep snow and ice, entering the camp over a boulder field. The linear campsite is on a windy shoulder on the mountain, with the tents protected by walls of stones. Water is available from the icy river that flows alongside.

  From Camp 1 to Camp 2 the elevation increases by over 750m, again a tough day's climb taking five to six hours. There is a col midway that makes a good resting point. This is often used as an intermediate campsite, commonly referred to as 'Camp One-and-a-half'. It has an expansive flat open area.

Rough trekking up the Relinchos Valley

91

Camp 2, like Nido de Condores, is the most popular rest site above Plaza Argentina. It is an open camp with little protection from the wind and sun. Fresh water flows through the icy river beside the camp. Above the camp-site, under a cliff face, is a grave to an Argentinean who died in 1983. The grave is rather shallow, and portions of his clothes and body are exposed.

From Camp 2 to **Rocas Blancas** is a mere three hours of an easy climb, occasionally over ice. The route is around the rear of the mountain. Crampons and an ice axe will be essential to negotiate the short ice field.

From Plaza Argentina to Camp 1 is a frustrating day through the penitentes

Many dispense with the last camp, preferring to sleep better at Camp 2 and make the summit attempt from there. However, a climb on summit day of 1355m, or double the previous days' climbs, is extremely

demanding. Going for the summit from Camp 2 means you have to stop and don crampons at the ice field, and take them off beyond it. This loses precious time on the most important day.

Rocas Blancas (also referred to as Piedras Blancas – small as opposed to large rocks) is an exposed site nestled against the white rocks from which it takes its name. There is no water.

A windswept Camp 2 at 5600m

The Route to the Summit

Rocas Blancas is on the Normal route above Camp Berlin. From Berlin there is an initial steep scramble before reaching the stony path. From Rocas Blancas the trail to the Normal route is good and easy. Where the trails meet the climb is steady to a col where there is a ruined wooden hut known as **Independencia** (6250m). Some climbers may opt to camp at Independencia and shorten summit day by a further hour or so. ▶

Independencia is a popular spot for a rest and a drink, perhaps also a convenient place to don crampons, depending on the weather.

The climb from Independencia is steady and traverses up to a ridge known as Cresta del Viento. Here you turn left to cross a very exposed area where the wind is unrelenting. Beyond the Cresta del Viento is the Gran Acarreo that leads to the base of the Canaleta. The Gran Acarreo is a relatively easy traverse, but the terrain becomes loose underfoot.

To classify the Canaleta as a slag heap is perhaps disingenuous, but most apt. The mixture of loose sand and gravel is frustrating, for with every two steps taken you slide back one. The Canaleta is 400m high and takes several hours to ascend. Near its base is a cliff face where

The route through the Gran Acarreo

climbers leave rucksacks, taking only the bare essentials to the summit. Here guides will encourage climbers to summon up all their remaining strength for this final assault.

View from the summit towards the south, with the Canaleta trail on the right

At the top of the Canaleta there is a gentle traverse to negotiate and some large boulders to overcome before arriving at the summit. Above this traverse the ridge is known as the **Cresto del Guanaco**, and connects the south summit to the north summit. On the north summit, the highest point of the Americas is marked by a simple aluminium cross.

Views from the summit can be stunning. To the southwest you can see the mountain of Tupungato. Below is the south face with the Horcones Inferior Glacier and Plaza Francia visible.

Almost every climber brings a memento of scarves, bandanas, flags and so on to the summit so that, by the end of the season, the tiny cross can hardly be seen. The ice and snow of the winter, however, is a natural clearer, and by spring the cross is restored to its isolation.

SUMMARY COMPARISONS

Item	Normal route	Vacas Valley route
Distance base camp	35km	42km
Distance to summit	Shorter	Longer, because of traverse around to Normal route
Difficulty	Easier, shallow rivers to cross	More difficult to base camp and Camp 2, deeper rivers to cross
Time	Shorter	At least a day longer each way
Water	None above base camp	Streams to Camp 2
Flora and fauna	Relatively barren	Greener, more flora and fauna
Interest	Lots of people	Fewer people, more interesting countryside
Cost	Cheaper	Add $US200 to Normal route cost for extra days

The Long Walk Out

Fast food café at Plaza de Mulas

Most trekkers will take a day to descend from Berlin to Plaza de Mulas. Similarly, a day is the usual time from

Rocas Blancas to Plaza Argentina. The Vacas Valley descent is much slower than the Normal route. The fields of *penitentes* make trekking slow, and many will reach base camp late in the day.

Although the climbing is over, and the air is becoming thicker, the day is a difficult one. All the gear that was taken up in loads on previous days must be taken down now in one go. Rucksack straps should be pulled tight into the chest to avoid back strain. Those arriving at the top camps will be pleasantly surprised to be offered excess food and fuel oil. Guides will bundle food and fuel and leave it for future visits.

The descent to Plaza de Mulas

On the track down stumbling and falling will be inevitable, and here the trekking poles provide good balance. The monotony will be broken by sudden surges as trekkers throw caution to the wind and virtually ski down the steeper gravelly paths.

The beer at base camp that was forbidden a week before, that was so expensive a week before, is drunk in copious amounts by descenders. The walk to the hotel next morning to make that phone call home now takes only a few minutes.

It is a long arduous day from Plaza de Mulas to the road head. The trekkers will look in envy at the arrieros on their horses. The care that was taken over the rivers on the way in will be ignored as the returning trekkers plunge recklessly into the water.

At Confluencia, where a well-earned rest is inevitable, it will be difficult to motivate the limbs to rise up and make that final effort to the road.

On the Vacas Valley route it is customary to make an overnight stop at Casa de Piedra, but many continue the 42km to Punta de Vacas.

Other Routes

The best of both worlds is to ascend via the Vacas Valley route and descend via the Normal route. This provides the time and difficulty to acclimatise on the Vacas Valley route, yet shortens the overall trip by a day. It also enables you to compare the two routes.

Vacas Valley ascent, Normal route descent ◀

The difficulty with changing the ascent and descent is that your gear left at base camp Plaza Argentina must be sent out to the road head and returned to Plaza de Mulas. However, if this arrangement is made with the guide or mule company before the start there should be no difficulty. Mules make the trips in and out and across every day. The other essential ingredient in changing over is that top camp must be at Rocas Blancas; otherwise it would be necessary to traverse over and back to Camp 2 to collect the tent and other gear.

There is a route from Confluencia via Plaza Francia to Plaza Argentina. This involves climbing up to 5100m over Port Relinchos, before descending into Plaza Argentina. The route is only possible when the level of

snow at Port Relinchos is comparatively low, so would require some advance information. It is a difficult ascent, but a most dangerous descent, so that a route out from Plaza Argentina to Confluencia is not an option.

Dropping off a load at Camp Canada

The Polish Glacier direct traverse ▶

The glacier is notoriously unstable and guides discourage this route. It is rare to see anyone on the glacier, but the route (with crampons) is direct and consequently much shorter.

From Camp 2 on the Vacas Valley route there is the direct ascent via the Polish Glacier.

There are three strategies for traversing the glacier – a wide sweep to the south to Piedra Bandera, a direct line across to the east ridge of Aconcagua, or a central traverse. The route via Piedra Bandera will be less steep than the central line and less prone to crevasses and seracs. Conversely, the direct line to the east ridge is over a 45° slope, and most prone to crevasses.

All the routes involve firstly climbing through the *penitentes* above Camp 2 on to the flat lower section of the glacier. The Piedra Bandera route is then to the left towards a large banded rock (6400m). From Piedra Bandera the route continues on the left side of the glacier, getting steeper and more prone to crevasses, onto the east ridge of Aconcagua. There are many false summits on the east ridge before the real summit is seen.

Skiing or snowboarding down the glacier to Camp 2 is more popular than climbing up.

Vacas Valley via Plaza Guanaco ◀

An alternative route via the Vacas Valley.

Instead of turning left at Casa Piedra the route continues following the Vacas river up through Quebrada Vieja Alta (high old valley).

Passing a disused refugio at 3435m you eventually arrive at an open area which is Plaza Guanaco (4000m). From base camp three intermediate camps will be necessary before the route meets the others above Independencia.

The Plaza Guanaco route needs a special permit costing $500 per person. The control office in Mendoza may disallow the passage because of the special amenity protection assigned to Quebrada Vieja Alta. No more than a few expeditions each year are sanctioned, generally accompanied by a ranger, with strict controls on waste.

PART III

TREKS IN THE ACONCAGUA AREA

Puente del Inca and Los Penitentes

The best approach is to get used to the altitude in a gradual manner. Before heading off on a major expedition check out the local scene. In and around Puente del Inca and Los Penitentes there are gentle, flat walks, and a few arduous ones to follow on with to help you acclimatise.

Andinistas graveyard
Along the road between Puente del Inca and Los Penitentes is a graveyard to those who have died in this area of the Andes. The graveyard is immediately beside the road, 2.5km from Los Penitentes and 3.5km from Puente del Inca. It is a sombre place, with many plaques of relatively recent origin.

Natural history museum
About 2km along the road from Los Penitentes east towards Punta de Vacas there is a former railway structure that has been converted into a small makeshift museum. This is a fun place, not to be taken too seriously. The owner (who speaks not a word of English) has used his skills to erect pumps and pulleys to show how volcanoes work. He has rock and mineral samples, and his paintings display the history of the Andes. An illustrated lecture tour (in Spanish, but most will get a good grasp) costs a few pesos.

There is on option of continuing the walk along the road towards Punta de Vacas. At a bend in the road, a few kilometres further on, there is a clear view through the valleys to Tupungato (6550m).

Ski slopes at Los Penitentes
There are treks up the mountain at Los Penitentes, following the cable car routes, leading up to 3727m at Cruz de

Trekking paths above Los Penitentes

Caña. The climb is steep, but there is no hurry, and plenty of rests can be taken.

Between Los Penitentes and Puente del Inca there is a steep valley where the Santa Maria stream descends out of the mountains. A trek into the valley and a turn to the west leads up to Puquios (3676m). Once again the climb is quite steep.

Following the Santa Maria stream further in leads to Bandera Norte (4200m), which gives a commanding view of the Horcones to Los Penitentes area.

Quebrada Blanca

Out of Puente del Inca on the south side there is a trek up to the top of Quebrada Blanca (4203m). The peak is also known locally as Banderita. The route is via the first valley to the left on the road towards Las Cuevas. It is a tough day-long trek, and there are no water sources.

A walk up to Cristo Redentor

Half-day trek	8km round trip
Dirt road	Max elevation 3800m
Total climb 700m	No water sources

This is a stiff walk intended as an introduction to the altitude. In the summer months, between January and March, the walk will be over dry ground. Outside these periods there may be snow. The area around the great statue is exposed and windswept, and warm gear is essential at all times. Trekking boots are recommended,

The Tolosa mountain viewed from Cristo Redentor

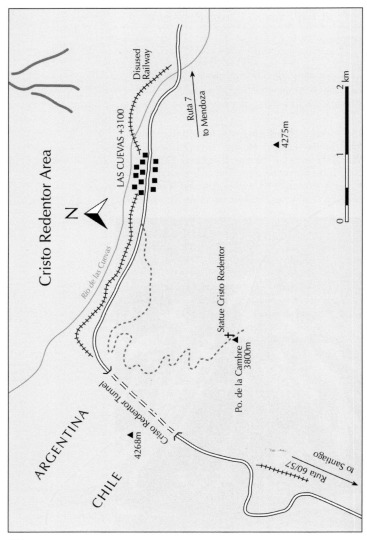

particularly for the descent. For those not acclimatised expect to take three hours for the ascent, and one hour coming down.

The statue of Christ the Redeemer was built overlooking the pass between Argentina and Chile, and the route to it is the old RN7 road (now replaced by the tunnel). It is accessible with a four-wheel drive vehicle in dry weather, but the route is tough and difficult, and deteriorates further every year.

To get to the old road you have to go to the village of **Las Cuevas** (3100m), 12km from Puente del Inca. The old road leads off to the south of the village under an arched building. Multiple hairpin bends wind up the hillside, and you wonder how cars and trucks coped with the climb in the not too distant past.

The trek is rewarding, however, as the col is a very interesting, ghostly place. An old stone building on one side welcomes travellers to Argentina, whilst close by is another that is clearly Chilean. The enormous statue has many plaques, the principal one signifying its importance as a symbol of peace between the two countries.

Across the valley is the imposing mountain of Tolosa with its high hanging glacier in the shape of a man with no legs – *el hombre coja*.

The easiest route down is along the steep spine that cuts through the road.

Horcones Valley to Plaza Francia

3–4 day trek	65km round trip
Varied terrain	Max elevation 5000m
Total climb 2420m	No water sources

The trek is in to the south face of Aconcagua and leads to a relatively high elevation. It is not difficult; the effort required is well worth the elevation gained and the visual reward is excellent.

Plaza Francia is an ill-defined camp near the south face. It is not necessary to travel all the way in to Plaza Francia to experience the wonderful vista of the south face and the Horcones Inferior Glacier; a stop at 4000m will achieve this. However, between 4000m and 5000m is an easy walk over good ground, and there are many suitable places to camp. Thus, the trekker can vary the distance travelled up the valley to suit his composure and condition.

The route follows the ruta Normal from the Horcones ranger station, in past the Horcones Lagoon and up to **Confluencia**. The first day of the trek is easy, and the 15km point will be reached in about three to four hours. From Confluencia the trail gets tougher, rising out of the relatively flat Horcones Valley around boulders and over rough, steep ground. After about two hours the valley widens and the trail is an even gradient over good ground, which stretches from 3500m to 5300m.

The south face of Aconcagua with the Horcones Inferior Glacier in the foreground

There are campsites 5km from Confluencia, not very far from clean water. In the main valley there are ample sheltered sites to pitch a tent. However, up in the valley there is no clean water. Sources of clean water near the

Detail of the hanging glaciers on Aconcagua's south face

south face are also difficult to locate, depending on the melted water from the face itself.

It is suggested that the first night is spent at Confluencia, the second at **Plaza Francia** or an intermediate site, and the third back at Confluencia. Alternatively, it is possible to trek from Confluencia up and back in one day. However, if there are climbers on the south face, it gives little time to watch them.

Plaza Francia is normally deserted, because the numbers attempting the south face are few. A ruined hut marks the original campsite. At Plaza Francia the enormity of Aconcagua can be experienced. The 3000m-high by 7000m-wide wall of rock, snow and ice is a daunting spectacle. With binoculars you can look up to the summit.

On the left the great Horcones Inferior Glacier creaks and groans as this living mass works its way down the valley.

TREKS AT VALLECITOS

Vallecitos Ski and Mountain Lodge

Vallecitos is one-and-a-half hours' drive from Mendoza, on the road towards Aconcagua. The centre operates transport from Mendoza and to Aconcagua.

Vallecitos is a convenient, practical and inexpensive centre to acclimatise for Aconcagua. This small ski resort is dedicated, during the summer months, to acclimatisation. It should be emphasised that the mountain lodge is small, generally only able to cater for 40 people, and that the facilities are very basic.

Vallecitos (2900m) can act as a camp for one-day or half-day treks, or as a base camp for two-to-four-day treks. From the centre there are short treks to 4000m and above, and longer treks to 5700m and even up to 6300m. Guided treks and mule services are available. Alternatively there is a campsite above the centre, near fresh water, with many choices of unguided treks.

The steep road to Vallecitos is off the Ruta 7, less than an hour from Mendoza towards Aconcagua. At Potrerillos a paved road to the left leads towards La Chacrita, then forks right to rise on a dirt track to Vallecitos.

The Vallecitos ski centre

The small ski centre is a motley collection of huts, all shut during the summer except for the lodge. Bedrooms have bunks, and there are four separate bathrooms. There

Vallecitos Area

Agustin
Alvarez
5400m

Quebrada del Salto

Refugio

Junción
5200m

Laguna

Cerro Colorado

Mausy
4800m

Lomas
Blancas
3500m

San Bernardo
4450m

Arenales
3500m

Quebrada de la Jaula

Rincon
5500m

VALLECITOS
TREK

El Salto
Camp 4050m

VALLECITOS
SKI
CENTRE

LOMAS
BLANCAS
TREK

Vallecitos
5770m

Río Vallecitos

Piedra
Grande Camp
3500m

Pico Vallecitos
5750m

Río Blanco

La Hoyada
Camp
4500m

Lomas
Amarillas
5300m

Pico Franke
5100m

to Mendoza

El Plata
6300m

Pico Plata
6100m

Qda de la Angostura

Negro 5800m

N

0   1   2
km

is hot water, a public telephone and barbecue facilities. At night a fire blazes in the dining room. There are no frills here – food is simple and basic, no carpets, central heating or television.

The campsite above the resort is at an elevation of 3200m on a flat area of open ground known as **Las Vegas** (the springs). Vallecitos is a popular area for hillwalkers and climbers at weekends. If it proposed to stay at the lodge, and/or to go on guided treks, it is advisable to book in advance.

Lomas Blancas

Half-day trek	9km round trip
Easy terrain	Max elevation 3850m
Total climb 950m	No water sources

This is an easy introductory climb. From the lodge cross the entrance road and take the route that goes east into a valley, and then turns north up through a narrow gorge. The path winds it ways up to a col. To the west of the col is the Lomas Blancas peak.

There are guanacos in these mountains, so keep a close watch. The peak itself is a rocky hilltop, with a simple metal cross at the summit.

The return can be via an ill-defined path that goes south from the summit over rock outcrops, eventually coming down over relatively steep ground onto the ski runs.

Cerro Vallecitos

4-day trek	37km round trip
Moderate terrain	Max elevation 5770m
Total climb 2870m	Water sources

This trek can be varied to suit the weather and the physical condition of the participants. The trek is up towards the snow-capped peaks where there are choices of how far to go and which peak to climb. The most popular choices, on non-technical routes, are:

- **Cerro Vallecitos** (5770m)
- **Pico Plata** (6100m)
- **El Plata** (6300m), beyond Pico Plata

The route is simple, and it would be difficult to go astray. From the rear of the lodge ascend to the northeast, up over the crest, following the river.

There are four campsites above the Vallecitos centre. The first is at **Las Vegas** on a flat grassy site (3200m). The second is at **Piedra Grande** (3500m), a short walk further into the valley. **El Salto** (The Jump) is three to four hours beyond Piedra Grande, via a narrow ravine and up over moraine. It is possible to trek from the ski centre to El Salto (4000m), with a full pack, in one day. At El Salto water depends on the degree of melting snow above, but generally the stream – Rio Vallecitos – is adequate.

Top camp is La Hoyada (The Pot, 4500m), four hours above El Salto. The route follows the stream as it bends up

The hostel can arrange to deliver a mule load to El Salto. This makes the first day's trek less onerous. Some provisions can be stored at El Salto, so that only the minimum is taken to La Hoyada.

Heavy snow near El Salto campsite

to the southwest. Underfoot the route is over loose moraine, steep in places. The campsite is sheltered inside an inverted cone-shaped area. Once again water is not too far away and is dependent on melted ice and snow from above.

Summit day to Cerro Vallecitos is arduous. The climb of over 1200m is a long day that should start before 4am. Initially the ground is loose scree, but this changes to firmer ground, over solid rock in some areas. For the first few hours the climb follows a winding path up to Lomas Amarillas. At the Plata Vallecitos col the route turns to the north, and underfoot the ground becomes harder. Cerro Vallecitos is a bare rock peak, quite exposed, with a steep trek to its summit.

The return to La Hoyada is a leisurely descent, though it will be very windy as far as the col. From **La Hoyada** back to the hostel can be comfortably achieved in one day.

The Cerro Vallecitos Summit is an exposed area of solid rock

PART IV

TUPUNGATO

Tupangato – the Andes' Great Mountain

To the mountaineers of Argentina and Chile the name 'Tupungato' evokes feelings not accorded to any other mountain. Many come to this area to climb Aconcagua – because it is high, they will say – but Tupungato epitomises what the Andes is all about. It is a long journey in from the road to get to Tupungato, but worth every step, especially if it is through the wilderness of Tupungato Provincial Park.

Tupungato (6550m) is a dormant volcano lying on the border between Chile and Argentina, just under 100km south of Aconcagua. It is the 12th highest mountain in the Americas. A volcanic eruption was recorded as recently as 1986, but this was on Tupungato's little sister, Tupungatito (5640m), a few kilometres to the south. There is no crater on Tupungato, but a smoking crater on

Tupungato from Portezuelo del Fraile (Friar's Col)

Matthias Zurbriggen
and Stuart Vines
were the first to
climb Tupungato in
1897. They were part
of the Aconcagua
expedition led by
Edward Fitzgerald.

Tupungatito. Tupungato has a near vertical face on its eastern side, some 2000m high, first climbed in 1985, but the two Argentinean climbers died on the descent on the southern side.

Tupungato attracts few climbers, virtually none from abroad. Even with the discovery of the crashed plane in its glacier (at which time the mountain received world recognition) the numbers of visitors has only slightly increased. This is most certainly due in part to its remoteness. ◄

THE MOUNTAIN, THE GLACIER, THE MISSING AEROPLANE AND THE LOST GOLD IN CONTEXT

A scheduled British South American Airways flight from Buenos Aires to Santiago mysteriously disappeared on 2 August 1947. The British Lancaster was named *The Stardust*, and had six passengers and a crew of four.

The colourful characters among its passengers fuelled speculation over its disappearance. One was a diplomat carrying secret documents from the British king. Relations between Britain and Argentina were tense, and it was considered that these documents, to be delivered to Santiago, were of particular importance. Another was a Palestinian who had a large diamond sewn into the lining of his coat. A German widow was returning to Chile with the ashes of her husband.

The plane had flown from Buenos Aires to Mendoza, and was over the Andes on the final leg of its journey. Its route was to circle around Aconcagua before landing in Santiago. The pilot radioed a message to Santiago reporting that all was well, despite a storm over the Andes, and that he expected to land in four minutes. A Morse-coded message was then received from the plane, spelling out the letters S T E N D E C. At 5.45 p.m. the plane disappeared, never to be heard of again.

Rumours spread fast. There were reports that the plane, a converted Lancaster bomber, was carrying a cargo of gold. The widow, with her little urn, was transformed into a Nazi spy.

Over 50 years later, on 26 January 1998, two young climbers from Buenos Aires, Pablo Reguera and Fernando Garmendia, were 4500m up on Tupungato when Pablo spotted part of an engine on the ground, with the words 'OLLS-ROYCE' inscribed on it.

British Lancaster of the 1940s

'How did they get a car up here?' Pablo mused. The two searched the area and found other objects, such as clothing, including pieces of a heavily pinstriped suit. However, the two climbers did not realise the significance of their find. They took no photographs, and made no record of the location. After a successful summit of Tupungato they descended, casually mentioning their find to the army ranger.

The ranger, Armando Cardozo, asked other climbers to look out for wreckage, but there were no more sightings. Nine months later Armando was having lunch with an enthusiast of lost planes, José Moiso, when he recalled the incident. José had been brought up near an airbase on the outskirts of Buenos Aires, and had a passion for lost planes and mountaineering. When he was a child one of his father's great stories was about the missing Lancaster with its valuable cargo. He had already surveyed the site of the wreck of a Fairchild FH22 plane, which crashed while carrying a team of rugby players.

José persuaded Cardozo, himself an accomplished climber, to accompany him on an expedition. They set off in March 1999, but were caught up in a violent storm, and had to retreat without ever finding the wreckage site. A year later José and Cardozo returned in the company of José's son, Alejo. They located the wreckage at 4800m. Thus began the search that resulted in a major army expedition of 100 soldiers and as many mules trekking up the mountain, and a flood of international reporters.

Scientific investigations established that the aircraft crashed due to navigational error. The pilot had radioed that he was ascending to 24,000ft to avoid a storm. In the clouds, with no landmarks (and in 1947 positioning systems were non-existent) he had calculated his course and position. He was unaware of a 300mph jet stream and thought he was on course to descend to Santiago when he crashed into Tupungato. The Lancaster hit the mountain and fell onto the glacier. A resulting avalanche covered it. The

Army ranger Armando Cardozo and mountaineer Pablo Reguera

glacier apparently swallowed up the wreckage and slowly carried it down the mountain, to emerge at its base 50 years later.

The fact that neither the gold nor the diamond were ever found continues to attract those with the energy and ability to search. Some documents have emerged, but disintegrated before it could be established if they related to important Anglo–Argentinean relations. Amongst the most amazing discoveries were the aircraft wheels, fully inflated. Ninety per cent of the wreckage is still buried in the glacier, which yields up a little more of its cargo every year. No one has ever solved the mystery of the Morse-coded S T E N D E C.

Armando Cardozo continues to act as a ranger in Tupungato. A most interesting, yet very modest man, he lives with his family in Tupungato town. He is an army sergeant based at La Plaza and regularly guides trekkers into the park. Pablo Reguera is an accomplished high mountain guide with a wonderful sense of humour. The two met again, for the first time since the initial encounter, in late 2003, and accompanied the author on the wilderness trek to Friar's Col, described below.

A report of the discovery of *The Stardust* was published in *The Observer* newspaper on Sunday, 24 March 2002. It can be found on *The Observer* website, www.observer.co.uk. The website www.pbs.org/wgbh/nova/transcripts/2802vanished.html contains a transcript of a documentary made for television entitled *Vanished*.

TUPUNGATO ROUTES

There are four recognised routes up Tupungato:
- The first (most popular) via Chile, following the **Rio Colorado**

Two from Tupungato town in Argentina:
- via the **Rio Azufre**
- via the **Portezuelo del Fraile (Friar's Col)**
- The fourth from Punta de Vacas in Argentina, via the **Rio Tupungato**

All the routes in Argentina go through the Tupungato Provincial Park.

TABLE OF TUPUNGATO ROUTES			
Route	Chile–Rio Colorado	Rio Azufre	Friar's Col	Rio Tupungato
Base camp	48km	50km	43km	75km
Mule trek	48km	40km	28km/35km	65km
Mule stop	Vegas del Flojo	Portezuelo Tupungato	Friar's Col	Portezuelo Tupungato
Permits	Difrol, Chilgener	Army	Army	None
Difficulties	River crossings	Few	Friar's Col Ascent/descent Rio de Las Tunas crossing	Few
Water	Treatment	Good	Generally clear	Good
Total time	12 days	13 days	12/14 days	14 days

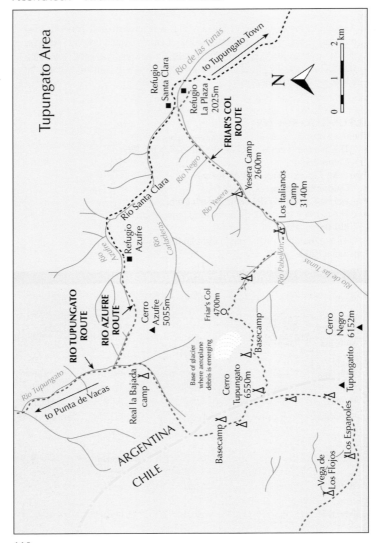

Tupungato Area

to Tupungato Town

Rio de las Tunas

Refugio
Santa Clara

Refugio
La Plaza
2025m

**FRIAR'S COL
ROUTE**

Rio Santa Clara

Rio Negro

Yesera Camp
2600m

Rio Yesera

Los Italianos
Camp
3140m

Refugio Azufre

Rio Azufre

Rio Cañaderas

Rio Pabellón

Rio de las Tunas

**RIO TUPUNGATO
ROUTE**

**RIO AZUFRE
ROUTE**

Cerro
Azufre
5055m

Friar's Col
4700m

Basecamp

Cerro
Negro 6152m

Rio Tupungato

to Punta de Vacas

Real la Bajada
camp

Base of glacier
where aeroplane
debris is emerging

Cerro
Tupungato
6550m

Tupungatito

Basecamp

ARGENTINA

CHILE

Vega de
Los Flojos

Los Españoles

N

0   1   2 km

The table above summarises the four routes. The distances to base camp include the distances that the mules can trek to. Thus, on the Rio Colorado route the mules go all the way to base camp. For the routes via Argentina it is necessary to carry all gear for a further 10km approximately. On the Friar's Col route the distance the mules can trek to is governed by the ground conditions – too much snow or ice and they have to abandon after 28km, 7km short – 7km that is steep and difficult – so that the total carry could be as long as 15km.

There is a complication. There are two Rio Azufre's, one on the Chilean side, the other on the Argentinean side. The Chilean Rio Azufre is a tributary of the Rio Colorado, it is a deep and difficult river crossing. On the Argentinean side the route follows that country's Rio Azufre, which joins the Rio de Las Tunas near the town of Tupungato.

All routes entail multiple river crossings. Via the Friar's Col there is a major crossing of the Rio de Las Tunas a few kilometres from the road head. The descent and ascent of Friar's Col is semi-technical, requiring ropes and helmet.

The Tupungato river valley from Punta de Vacas

Via Rio Azufre and Friar's Col it is necessary to hire mules from the army. The army service is excellent. They will accommodate and feed the trekkers at the road head, make great fires, take good care of the mules and act as guides. However, the service is slow and very expensive.

The routes to the summit via Rio Colorado and Friar's Col join on the mountain to ascend on the southern side of Tupungato. The other two routes join to ascend on the northern side of the mountain.

The route via Chile and Rio Colorado

The shortest, and the most popular, route up Tupungato is on the Chilean side via Rio Colorado.

Many guides and expedition operators in Santiago will organise the trek. Two permits are required, but there is no fee. In Santiago, on Bandera 52, the first of these permits is obtained from Dirección de Fronteras y Limites (DIFROL). The electricity company that operates the power station on the Rio Colorado will issue the second permit: go to Chilgener, located at Miraflores 222. ◀

From Santiago the route is via the Cajón de Maipo, southeast of Santiago, through Las Vizcachas, La Obra and El Manzano. Around 20km of dirt track road leads to Los Maitenes where mules can be hired, then another 20km leads up to the start of the trek at Chacayal. Public buses do not go in to Chacayal. ◀

Survival tip: The sequence of obtaining the permits in Santiago for Tupungato is important. DIFROL should be the first stop. They will give a note and directions to Chilgener.

There are good places to camp at Chacayal. The trail is along the right-hand, southern bank of the Rio Colorado, crossing minor streams. The first campsite is beside the **Rio Museo** (2400m). Known as **Baños Azules**, this lies under the peak of Pan de Azucar (Bread of Sugar).

The second day is a trek to **Vega de los Flojos** (3300m), a tough climb of 900m. But first there is the Rio Azufre to negotiate. The water will be knee-deep and the current strong. Expect a good wetting that will require a change of socks/boots/trousers. You have the option of a prearranged trip by mule over the river, but the wade through the surging waters is more exciting. The trek from Rio Museo to Vega de los Flojos will take six to eight hours. If this day's trek is too long it is possible to camp at **Piedra Azul** (3100m). Piedra Azul (also referred to as Agua Azul) provides the first sight of the summits of Tupungato and Tupungatito.

Vega de los Flojos (spring of the loose rocks/ground) is a green area, somewhat similar to Piedra Numerada on the El Plomo trek. The water from the spring must be treated.

For those better acclimatised the first camp can be made at 3200m, then on to base camp at 4700m. Another camp is made before the summit attempt from top camp at 5800m. However, most climbers spread the ascent from Vega de los Flojos over three days. The trail is well defined and the campsites are recognisable by circles of rocks.

The first of these campsites is **Los Espanoles** (4000m). There is no water available here. Around 300m higher is a better campsite near high *penitentes*. Yet another campsite is available at 4600m, another at 5200m, at 5500m and finally at 5800m.

Tupungato Provincial Park

On the Argentinean side the Tupungato Provincial Park (170,000ha) stretches along the Chilean border south of

Tupungato Provincial Park (there are guanacos in the distance at the base of the left slope)

the Mendoza-to-Santiago road. Much more extensive than the Aconcagua Provincial Park (150,000ha), it is a wild, remote region. Herds of guanacos roam freely. Condors soar overhead.

Access to the southern side of the park is usually via the road south from Mendoza, the RN 40, and turning right onto the RP 86 to the town of Tupungato, a journey of 80km. There are daily buses from Santiago to Tupungato town. From the road, looking across the plain, there is a spectacular view of the Andes from the Frontal Cordillera with El Plata (6300m) to the Principal Cordillera and Tupungato (6550m). ◄

It is necessary to obtain permission from the army to enter the park. The army camp in Tupungato issues the permit, which is free. From the camp it is 35km over dirt road to where the road divides – to the left and south **Refugio La Plaza**, to the right and north **Refugio Santa Clara**. There are three refugios in this area, all initially intended as hostels for trekkers, now all army camps. Refugio Plaza is the nearest to Tupungato town and the starting point for the trek via Friar's Col. Over the Rio de las Tunas, a few kilometres further on, is Refugio Santa Clara. The dirt track carries on past Santa Clara for a further 20km to **Refugio Azufre**, the starting point for the trek via Rio Azufre.

Tupungato is a charming, friendly town has much to offer the traveller – trekking, horse trekking, wineries, fly fishing, to name but a few. Above all else it is a peaceful place. At an elevation of 1050m it is not quite as warm as Mendoza, and is subject to snow in the winter. There are two good and inexpensive hotels, both on the main street, with the tourist office in the foyer of one of them.

The Rio de las Tunas leads towards Cerro Negro

Wilderness trek to Friar's Col

5–7 day trek	70km round trip
Varied terrain	Max elevation 4700m
Total climb 2675m	Water sources

The goal is to climb to an elevation of 4700m at the Portezuelo del Fraile (Friar's Col), a prominent vantage point from which there are spectacular views of Tupungato and its glacier, and a panorama of the Andes over to Aconcagua. The route can also be used to climb Tupungato itself (provided you are prepared for the descent and subsequent ascent of Friar's Col). ▶

Transport must be arranged from the town of Tupungato (where a permit must be obtained from the army camp) to Refugio La Plaza. If mules have been hired from the army they will arrange transport to the refugio. The army will offer the options of delivering a load to the first or second campsite, taking trekkers in by mule, guiding them and taking them out, or providing pack mules

It is highly unlikely that anyone else will be encountered on this trek – only a few parties per annum seek a permit. Wild guanacos will be seen quite often; condors and many other birds, lizards and mice, possibly a fox, are all most likely. A fire can be lit every night; there is plenty of water and good places to camp. Binoculars will be valuable for locating guanacos and condors, and for picking out pieces of the crashed aeroplane when looking across from Friar's Col to Tupungato.

Negotiating the rocks over the River Pabellón

and a ride to a point on the trail. The option of hiring a mule only from the army is not likely to be acceptable.

At La Plaza (2025m) the soldiers will be welcoming, probably offering food and accommodation. What is possibly more important is to ask for a ride over the Rio de Las Tunas. This fast-flowing river is down a gorge, and must be crossed at the start of the trek.

Day 1

Following the right-hand bank of the river, through the gorge, the route leads over a grassy plain and up into the valley. The snow-capped peak ahead is Cerro Negro (6152m). The river is murky, a faded orange colour. ◀

The **Yesera** camp is 10km from La Plaza at an elevation of 2600m. It is found immediately after crossing a stream (Quebrada Yesera, where there is clear water). Look out for a landmark concrete slab and a timber upright – the remnants of a former refugio built in the days of Juan Peron. There will be a store of firewood near the designated fireplace.

If 10km on the first day is inadequate then the second campsite is 15km further on, with an alternative site yet a further 5km. ◀

Day 2

The trail continues along the right-hand bank of the Rio de las Tunas until it meets the Rio Pabellón. Now the Pabellón takes on the orange colour, and comes down from a valley to the right. Beyond the junction of the two rivers it is necessary to cross to the left-hand bank, where camp **Los Italianos** is situated (3140m). The snow-capped peak up ahead is Cerro Pabellón (6100m). Firewood can be found up the hills. Around the camp there are tufts of bright green dense vegetation, some turning brown. This is yareta, which turns brown when it dies, and makes good fuel for the fire. The water from the river is murky but drinkable.

The energetic may decide to proceed past Los Italianos to a campsite 5km further on. **Casa del Cura** nestles under an overhanging rock, affording good shelter if the weather is bad.

The route over the next few days will be to *follow the orange river*, and when a fork in the river is encountered *take the right-hand branch*. This will lead eventually up to the Friar's Col. The colour of the water is due to sulphur (azufre) deposits further up the mountain.

Please note that it is the custom in Tupungato always to leave behind an adequate stock of firewood so that trekkers arriving late in the day do not have to search in the dark. So, even if the stock is high, replenish it.

Day 3

This is guanaco day, so tread lightly and have zoom lenses at the ready. The route is along the left bank of the Rio Pabellón until it meets the Rio Ancha, then turns right up Arroyo de la Quebrada Ancha (stream of the wide valley). The trail becomes steeper and the start of the col can be seen ahead. It is wise to be prepared, for the col continues for 7–8km up to the vantage point.

A camp can be made before the first step of the col (3600m) or, if the weather is kind, up above the first step (4200m). The first step is steep and may be covered in snow, in which case crampons are required. Above this first step there is no water and no firewood.

Day 4

From below the first step of the col to the vantage point takes four to five hours and two hours back. Just a daypack is required. Passing through the long windy col over rocky ground will be slow. The dip in the ridge up ahead is the vantage point (4700m). There is even a place to pitch a tent here, though it would be extremely windy.

The start of Friar's Col is steep and may be covered in snow

The view from Friar's Col back down Tupungato Provincial Park

There is no view of Tupungato or any other mountain until you reach the vantage point, where suddenly an amazing vista opens up over the awesome mass of Tupungato. The glacier that conceals the remains of the crashed Lancaster can be clearly seen, and it is obvious how difficult it would be to find a diamond at the foot of the glacier – which is 8km long and perhaps 2km wide. Off to the northwest is Aconcagua; between it and Tupungato is El Plata (6300m).

The descent down Friar's Col is 200m of an almost vertical drop over loose rock. A pair of helmeted climbers, alternating with a rope, could manage to descend, but the subsequent ascent with a heavy pack would be difficult and dangerous.

Days 5 & 6
The route back to La Plaza is retraced and can comfortably be achieved in two days.

PART V

SANTIAGO

Santiago City

A third of the population of Chile, some 5 million people, live in this sprawling metropolis. The centre of the city is compact – it is easy to orientate yourself – and has an excellent underground metro. The outer suburbs, however, are disjointed and it is remarkably easy to get lost.

Santiago is more complex in layout than Mendoza. The Rio Mapocho carves the city in two in an east–west direction. The main street is Avenida del Libertador Bernardo O'Higgins (commonly known, as in Mendoza, as the Alameda). The great liberator, O'Higgins, named it thus when he ordered the planting of trees to form a French-style boulevard.

At the lowest point of the curve of the Rio Mapocho is Baquedano, which may be considered the city's hub.

On a clear morning Santiago, viewed from the west, is dwarfed by the snow-capped cordillera of the Andes. During winter, however, it is one of the most polluted cities in the world, because the mountains can prevent smog clearance.

Street scene in the centre of Santiago

The road that goes west is the Pan American route towards Valparaiso. To the north is the airport and Argentina, and on the east lie the Andes.

Every hotel reception has city maps. The bustling, mainly pedestrianised, city centre lies to the north of the Alameda, between the metro stations of Universidad de Chile and Santa Lucia.

Public transport

Public transport in and around Santiago is excellent. The long-distance buses arrive from Mendoza at Los Heroes station. From here there is a metro throughout the city and other bus connections to outer areas. It is much more convenient, and of course cheaper, to see Santiago and its nearby attractions by public transport than by hiring a car and braving the traffic. Chilean drivers are undisciplined, swerving in and out of lanes and generally driving too fast.

The Santiago metro plan is in the shape of the Greek letter π, with three lines (although they are numbered 1,2 and 5). Los Heroes is at one junction, whilst Baquedano is at the other. Line no 4 is under construction and will circle the city to the southeast. Like all metros the directions are given as the last station on the line. The cost of a metro trip is $US0.3 (30 cents), irrespective of the distance.

For the mountaineer there are at least seven gear shops in the city with everything that might be required for an expedition. The costs are higher than in Mendoza, and hiring gear is not an option. Unlike Mendoza there is no closure of businesses for siesta in Santiago.

Survival tip

Making international calls from hotels is very expensive. Most Internet cafés provide a service that is 20 per cent of the cost, and there are specialist telephone call centres that are 10 per cent of hotel costs. These telephone call centres are generally at metro stations, for instance in the metro of Universidad de Chile.

In and Around Santiago

A trip from Baquedano north through Bellavista and up to the heights of San Cristobal (by funicular railway) is worthwhile. There is a good view of the city and the Andes from here. The zoo is en route.

Near metro station Cal y Canto, beside the river, there is the marvellous Mercado Central (Central Market). In the enormous steel-supported hall there is a wonderful fish restaurant. Not open in the evenings it is full every lunchtime, especially on Sundays, accommodating up to 800 customers. The menus include fish perhaps never seen in Western restaurants. All around are endless stalls selling fresh fish, fruit and vegetables.

The El Plomo Inca mummy (or at least a replica of it – see page 130) can be seen in the Museo de Historia Natural in the Quinta Normal Park, off Matacana (metro to Estación Central). It should be noted that some are sceptical of the authenticity of the mummy, given that it was found in prime condition on such a well-visited mountain so close to the city, and only discovered in 1954.

A good centre to buy gifts for home is Plaza Artesanos de Manquehue, a series of small shops in a covered market on Manquehue Sur, off Ave Apoquindo near Las Condes. Lapis lazuli is Chile's semi-precious stone, and necklaces, earrings, cuff links in silver and gold can be purchased here or in Bellavista. The airport shops charge roughly double.

From the junction of Alameda and Ahumeda in Santiago buses regularly go to the Maipo Valley. This long, picturesque valley stretches some 70km into the mountains. There are small wineries for tasting, places to stop and purchase honey, cider and crafts en route, and at the top of the valley there are hot springs (see also the El Morado trek, page 133).

At the start of the Maipo Valley is the vineyard of Concha y Toro. Entrance is free, and it is a most rewarding experience. The best time to visit is at 10am when it is cool and there is an English language tour. Each participant is given a free tasting glass, allowed to sample three

Replica of the El Plomo mummy

The Pacific Ocean at Vina del Mar near Valparaiso

top wines and taken through the vineyard and its cellars. Concha y Toro is renowned for the quality of its *carmanére reserva*.

Many of Chile's notable wineries are not as easily accessible as in Mendoza. Undurraga, one of the oldest and most prestigious, however, is only 35km away, at Melipilla on the road towards San Antonio, southwest of Santiago. Their dessert wine, referred to as 'late harvest', is particularly delicious.

A one-and-a-half-hour bus journey from the bus station at the University of Santiago takes you to Valparaiso and the coastal resort of Vina del Mar. It can be particularly refreshing to take a walk by the sea after weeks in the mountains. Valparaiso is a quaint port town with 15 old funicular railways. On Sundays there is an enormous flea market.

CHILEAN RODEO

Every weekend throughout the summer there are rodeos in or near Santiago. To attend one is to witness a part of the life of Chile. For the purists Rancagua, the city some 90km south of Santiago, is the home of the Chilean rodeo, and draws the biggest crowds. However, the rodeos in and around Santiago give a good flavour of the occasion. In the Friday and Saturday press details of the rodeos are listed in the sports events for the weekend. The rodeo season begins in September, with qualifying events, and finishes with regional finals, semi-finals and the grand final in March.

This rodeo is quite different from its North American counterpart. The Chilean version is essentially about horsemanship. There is no wrestling with bulls or bringing calves to earth. Huasos, elegantly dressed with wide-brimmed hats, ponchos and high boots, and working in pairs, chase and control young cows using only their horses. There are no ropes, no whips, and no animal abuse. This is a display of skill and elegance. The judges award points for dressage and for the efficiency with which the Huasos control the cows.

Huasos at the rodeo

TREKS NEAR SANTIAGO

El Morado Valley

Half-day walk	15km round trip
Easy terrain	Max elevation 2450m
Total climb 650m	Water sources

Walking shoes only are required on this trek, which is at a relatively low altitude. El Morado is a national park within the Maipo Valley, and this walk is popular with Santiaginos at the weekends. The walk leads through a picturesque valley, with many campsites, past natural springs, lots of flowers, particularly orchids, up to a glacier.

Transport to El Morado during weekdays must be arranged. At weekends there are early morning minibuses (7am) from Plaza Italia. Public buses go up the Maipo Valley, but stop short of Baños Morales, where the walk starts. The La Cumbre gear shop on Apoquindo in Santiago is associated with an outdoor sports centre,

El Morado Valley with springs in the foreground and Cerro Morado at 4500m defining the end of the valley

Refugio Valdes, which is located at Baños Morales, and may be able to help. This centre, incidentally, not only arranges treks, but also offers a full range of outdoor activities including horse trekking, fossil hunting, rock climbing and mountain biking.

Through the Maipo Valley, passing sports and recreation areas, wineries, waterfalls and stunning countryside, the road goes through San José de Maipo onto a dirt track to branch off for Baños Morales. The lukewarm springs in the village are worth a visit.

There is a fee of $US2.5 into the park, payable to the ranger at the entrance. Initially the path is steep, but then levels to an even gradient. En route one cannot fail to notice the profusion of flowers, orchids and calandrinias being particularly plentiful. A drink from the sulphur springs beside the path will refresh (just a little – the taste may linger). The path eventually leads into a flat campsite beside a number of lagoons.

Cerro Morado is the jagged peak at the end of the valley. It has an altitude of 4500m, and to its left is Cerro San Francisco (4350m), with a glacier that sweeps down to discharge its morainic load beside the path. The altitude here is 2450m.

La Campana National Park

La Campana is a national park that lies between Santiago and Valparaiso. It is part of the coastal cordillera ridge of mountains. The dominant peak that can be seen from every part of the park is Cerro La Campana (1880m).

A visit to this national park can be considered under two possible categories:

- a gruelling 1400m climb over granite rock in the hot sun; or
- a sightseeing walk through a forest where there are many rare Chilean palms

Whichever option is chosen the park is an enjoyable day trip from Santiago. There are many species of birds and plants in this wildlife sanctuary.

There are two separate entrances to La Campana National Park. If it is proposed to climb the peak the entrance near **Olmué**, on the western side, should be used. From this side no palms will be seen.

Near **Ocoa**, on the northern side, there is a second entrance that is close to the palms, but two days' trek to Cerro La Campana. Ocoa is one-and-a-half hours by car from Santiago, and two-and-a-half hours by public bus. Olmué is two hours by car and three hours by public bus. The buses to Ocoa stop approximately 2km short of the park entrances. Buses from San Borja near Estacion Central in Santiago go very close to the Olmué entrance.

At both entrances there are clear maps displaying the various trails through the forest, where the palms are and where the campsites are located. An entrance fee of $US2.5 is payable, with an additional cost to camp. ▶

One of the very early visitors to La Campana was Charles Darwin in 1834. He climbed Cerro La Campana (on a cool winter's day) and was overwhelmed by the 360° vista of the Pacific Ocean around to the Andes.

The Chilean palm was widespread in central Chile until it was discovered that it contained a vast store of delicious treacle. Felling of the trees was set upon with a will and, as a result, it became almost extinct. It is now protected, and La Campana is the only significant surviving source. The massive trunks are often compared to elephant's legs, and very small coconuts are produced. The humming bird and the inquisitive truca, with its distinctive call, flourish in this natural habitat.

El Plomo

4–5 day walk	40km round trip
Varied terrain	Max elevation 5430m
Total climb 2400m	Water sources

Cerro el Plomo, translated as 'The Mountain of Lead', is the nearest 5000m peak to Santiago, and its white-capped summit can be seen from all parts of the city. The name comes from the deposits of lead that were mined in the area.

This non-technical climb is the most popular in Chile, attracting thousands every season. No permit is required, and no permissions necessary from any source; neither is it essential to hire a guide. The route is clear and the dangers are few. Invariably there will be others on the mountain.

As part of preparations for Aconcagua El Plomo has much to offer:

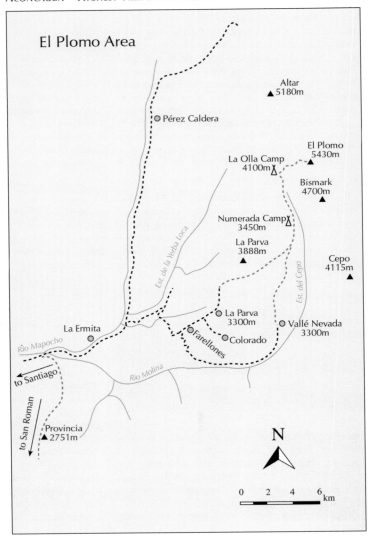

- the ground conditions are very similar for both mountains
- crampons will be required to cross the glacier near the summit
- summit day is a long arduous day, with possibly 1330m of climbing

The El Plomo trek takes four to five days' round trip from Santiago. Those with some acclimatisation will have no difficulty on a four-day, or possibly even a three-day, trek. For those preparing for Aconcagua or Tupungato an extra day at altitude will be most beneficial.

A number of operators organise guided expeditions up El Plomo, complete with mules. Indeed, some offer the package of El Plomo and Aconcagua as two peaks in two countries, with El Plomo intended as acclimatisation for Aconcagua. It is the custom with some of these operators to concentrate the expedition into four days, so that the summit day includes the trek back to the first camp. This is too onerous, even for those acclimatised.

The El Plomo peak in the evening over the Santiago suburb of Las Condes

The Inca mummy

At a height of 5200m there is an Inca altar, constructed of dry stone with an enclosure beside it. Two hundred metres above the altar, on the summit plateau, there are three rectangular enclosures. The congealed body of a small boy was discovered in one of them in 1954. The body was dressed in fine fabrics of vicuna and alpaca, and wrapped in a blanket. His hair was braided, and on his feet were fine leather moccasins. It is thought that he was a sacrifice to the Inca gods. A replica of the mummified remains can be seen in the Museo de Historia Natural in Santiago.

The mountain lies 20km to the north-east of Santiago, and is accessed via the valley of the Mapocho river.

The route to El Plomo ◄

There are two alternative starting points for El Plomo, both at ski resorts, both at approximately the same altitude,

There is a hotel at the start of the El Plomo trek at Valle Nevada

and both requiring a car for access. Public buses go from the centre of Santiago (Escuela Militar metro station, or Alameda) via Las Condes towards Barnecha. However, these buses will not travel in far enough to the trail head. If a group is going a shared taxi will be economical. For those on their own there is a custom of hitching in the area, which will be much more successful at weekends.

The route out of Santiago is via Las Condes and the rather affluent suburb of Vitacura, then into the Mapocho Valley, passing the exclusive houses of Arrayan. The starting point at **La Parva** ski resort is on the road beyond Farallones. For the **Valle Nevada** starting point the road rises steeply after the copper mine, and after numerous hairpin bends arrives at one of Chile's most popular ski centres. At both ski resorts there are hotels, one of which remains open throughout the year. These hotels cater for day-trippers and those seeking peace and relief from the heat of Santiago. They are expensive.

The trails from both starting points join together after a few kilometres to become one trail in to the first campsite. The mules leave from beside the hotels.

Day 1

Whether from La Parva or Valle Nevada the route begins at an altitude of 3300m. In the summer it will be possible for the delivery car or truck to go up the ski roads to shorten the first day's trek, but this may not be such a good policy for those seeking acclimatisation. The trek in to the first campsite at **Piedra Numerada** is a mere three hours, initially over steep ground, levelling off and then falling into the camp. From Valle Nevada the route goes directly up the ski slopes, around various reservoirs, following the main river valley.

Piedra Numerada is at an elevation of 3450m, not much height gain from the ski centre. It is on an open plain, beside the Molina river, and there is room for more than 50 tents. Cerro El Plomo can be seen clearly up the valley. To the right, dominating the campsite, is Cerro Bismarck. At 4700m the climb up Bismarck is very steep and demanding, but non-technical.

The campsite at Piedra Numerada with El Plomo in the background

In front of Piedra Numerada there are refreshing springs. Around the mighty boulder in the centre of the camp a drystone wall has been constructed that makes an excellent kitchen. There are plenty of sierra thrushes and wrens about the camp, and the perdicitas call to each other all day.

Day 2

From Piedra Numerada to the second campsite at **La Olla** (The Pot) is a three-hour walk over uneven moraine. The landscape becomes bleak and barren, with few plants and even fewer birds. En route there are the remains of an Inca enclosure.

Where to make camp at La Olla is a big decision. The best site is beside the orange **Refugio Federación** – no more than a tent-size wooden box – at 4100m. There is a water source here, the ground is flat and there is ample wind protection. However, it is still 1330m to the summit, a mighty climb for one day.

All sites above Federación are devoid of water. The first is La Olla itself, over the moraine ridge and down to a level of 4200m – hardly worth the effort.

At 4300m there is a small, sheltered site with room for six tents. It is on the trail up the mountain. Finally, at 4600m, beside a dilapidated timber hut, **Refugio Agostini**, there are a few spaces for tents, but the site is very exposed. In calm weather this site would be a good option.

A day acclimatising at La Olla may pay dividends, but any site above Federación is confined and could be exposed and windy.

Day 3/4

From Federación or La Olla summit day should commence at 3–4am. This is aimed at a midday summit when the weather conditions tend to be more favourable. Since the climb will start in darkness it is good practice to become acquainted with the early part of it the previous evening.

Initially the route is easy. The approach to Agostini, however, is over loose scree (*acarreo*). Leaving Agostini

Before dawn breaks on summit day a look back at the lights of Santiago will make for a welcome pause.

the ground improves slightly, but then deteriorates to resemble Aconcagua's Canaleta. The scree underfoot is weak and makes climbing frustrating.

The degree of snow on the mountain will dictate the difficulty of the ascent to the site of the altar. Over a slope that is sheltered from the sun, compact snow or ice may require crampons, but will be easier to climb. If there is no snow or ice the ground underfoot will be loose. The site of the sacrifice altar is a moving experience. One imagines the trauma on the mountain, 500 years ago, when a family gave up their little son for the common good.

From the altar to the summit is a climb in crampons over the glacier. It is possible to shorten the time on the glacier by a roundabout route over stony ground – either

The last hour of the El Plomo climb is over a glacier in crampons

Delight and relief at the summit of El Plomo

way the climb is over an hour, although at first sight it looks like half of this. There is a relatively flat ridge along the summit plateau of El Plomo several hundred metres in length. A simple wooden cross marks the highest point, from which stunning views may be available of Tupungato (6550m), Marmolejo (6110m) and Aconcagua (6962m).

Day 4/5

An early start the day after summit day allows adequate time to get back to the ski resort and into Santiago by nightfall. The walk is long and the final climb over the hills to the ski slopes will be taxing after the previous day's exertions. The hotel at the ski resort is quite used to serving dirty, unshaven climbers.

Provincia and San Ramón

Along the road towards El Plomo, just before the bridge over the Mapocho, Puente Ñilhue, there is a sign, Camino de Naranjo, pointing to the south. This is the start of a trail that goes over Cerro Provincia (2751m), and on to Cerro San Ramón (3249m). It is five hours' trek from the road to the top of Cerro Provincia, and another five hours to the summit of Cerro San Ramón.

These are obviously serious climbs that will necessitate camping, and will require heavy backpacks to be taken from 1100m at the road up to these peaks. On a cool day, however, it is possible to climb and descend in one day. The route is well marked out. Be advised, however, that there are a few false summits before the top.

From either of these peaks there should be, subject to weather conditions, good views of the city, probably giving a good impression of the smog that the Andes manages to trap.

PART VI
USEFUL INFORMATION

Maps, guidebooks and further reading

The availability of accurate ordnance maps of Aconcagua is poor, and there were none at all until 2003. The campsites at Plaza de Mulas and Confluencia have been moved, and bridges built in recent years. Older maps may not show them accurately. The outline of glaciers on older maps no longer reflects the real situation on the ground.

At the permit office in Mendoza you can buy a photomap, published by the Instituto Geografico Militar, that shows the mountain from the air and denotes the various sites, but the quality is poor. In 2003 they also published a map of Aconcagua that sells for $5.

The equivalent institute of geography in Santiago, Chile, on the other hand, with the same name, is an excellent establishment, where accurate ordnance maps can be purchased. It is located at Diecocho 369, opposite the Toesca metro.

The best map of Aconcagua is issued by Inka Expediciones, and sells at $15.

A 1:50,000 map of Aconcagua is published by Cordee, Leicester, England. The map shows the Normal route only, but its accuracy has been questioned.

The South American Explorers Club publishes a small map in black and white, entitled *Aconcagua – Summit of the Americas* by Ed Darack. It has useful data, but is a poor substitute for a proper map.

Omni Resources publish four old ordnance maps that would have to be cut up and put together, but these cost over $120 plus postage and are not up-to-date. Photocopies of the same maps – a much cheaper option – are available from Segemar (Servicio Geologico Minero Argentino).

There is only one other guidebook to Aconcagua – R.J.Secor's *Aconcagua, A Climbing Guide*, published by The Mountaineers in the USA (first

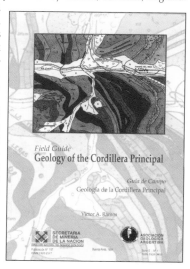

Field Guide
Geology of the Cordillera Principal

Guía de Campo
Geología de la Cordillera Principal

Victor A. Ramos

published 1994). The book has many black-and-white photographs.

The Bradt Trekking Guide to Chile and Argentina by Tim Burford contains a nine-page chapter on Aconcagua.

Franz Schubert and Malte Sieber, both German climbers living in Chile, are authors of *Adventure Handbook – Central Chile* (2002), documenting 23 trekking tours in the Chilean Andes. This excellent book is published by Viachile Editores (email malte@contactchile.cl), and may not be readily available in the West.

The Rough Guides are excellent publications for getting around countries such as Chile and Argentina: *The Rough Guide to Argentina* by Danny Aeberhard, Andrew Benson and Lucy Phillips (2000); *The Rough Guide to Chile* by Melissa Graham (2003).

Wayne Bernhardson is the author of a very good guide to Chile, part of the Moon Handbooks series.

Although it may be hard to get hold of, *The Highest Alps – A Record of the First Ascent of Aconcagua and Tupungato, and the Exploration of the Surrounding Valleys,* by E. A. Fitzgerald (1899), published by Methuen, is a wonderful study of the area, despite its age.

The Secretaria de Mineria de la Nacion in Argentina published a brief paper in English by Victor Ramos: *Geology of the Cordillera Principal* (1994). A larger, comprehensive treatise on geology, *Geologica de la Region de Aconcagua* (by the same author), was published in Spanish by Dir Nac De Servicio Geologica (1996).

Medicine for Mountaineers by James Wilkerson is published by The Mountaineers (1992). The Mountaineers also publish *Mountain Sickness* by Peter Hackett (1980). *The Use of Diamox in the Prevention of Acute Mountain Sickness* by Frank Hubble was published in The Wilderness Medicine Newsletter (March/April edition, 1995).

Guides and mountain services

The Mendoza local government website on Aconcagua has a list of companies who provide guides and services within the national park.

- Alessio Expediciones
- Andesport
- Aymara Expediciones
- Aconcagua Express
- Campo Base
- Fernando Grajales
- Geotrek
- La Gran Montana
- Gabriel Cabrere
- Hotel Plaza de Mulas
- Juan Herrera
- Inka Expediciones
- Malku
- Rudy Parra

Two Chilean companies, Azimuth360 and Andes Mountain Expediciones, are very experienced on Aconcagua and have good reputations.

The three largest expedition operators are Fernando Grajales, Aymara and Inka Expediciones. Grajales, a renowned former climber, now in his 70s, was the first to set up services on Aconcagua. With a stock of over 90 mules he provides a range of commercial services, including mules and the hire of mess tents, complete with cooks. Grajales hires guides to suit his bookings. In recent times his son has turned the business into a more efficient and professional company.

Aymara is a large company providing leisure and entertainment services throughout Argentina, hiring mules and guides to fit their needs. Aymara will carry gear, so that the climber only has to carry his small daypack. This may seem something of a luxury, but can be counterproductive in the acclimatisation process. The only time when a porter is valuable is on the descent to base camp.

Inka Expediciones has a stock of over 60 mules, and a permanent team of top-class guides. Whereas many of Grajales' guides and some of Aymara's are accomplished, but not licensed, Inka appears to be very particular, only employing guides who are licensed. Inka is being audited by the international mountain leader organisation UIAGM, the first company on Aconcagua to do so. In preparing for an expedition Inka's response time was found to be excellent.

Checklist of essential kit

CLOTHES

City clothes
Sun hat
Shorts (1pr)
Light T-shirt (2pr)
Trousers (1pr – for evenings)
Briefs (2pr)
Socks (2pr)
Shoes (1pr)

Approach trek
Wide-brimmed hat
Bandana
T-shirt
Shorts (1pr)
Vest
Briefs (1pr)
Trekking trousers (1pr)
Runner's tights (1pr – optional)
Trekking boots
Sock liners (2pr)
Waterproof jacket

High mountain
Light balaclava
Heavy balaclava
Woollen/fleece hat
Base layer shirts (2)
Base layer trousers (1 pr)
Fleece shirts (2)
Fleece trousers (1pr)
Briefs (2pr)
Wind bloc fleece
Down jacket
Waterproof trousers
Sock liners (2pr)
Fleece/woollen socks (2pr)
Gaiters
Thin inner gloves (1pr)
Fleece gloves
Down mittens

GEAR

General
Satchel
35-litre rucksack
Walking poles
Head torch, spare batteries
Category 4 sunglasses
-18°C sleeping bag
Thermarest/mattress
1-litre steel flask/thermos
1-litre water bottle
1-litre pee bottle

Mountain
70+ litre rucksack
Crampons
Spare pair sunglasses
Ice axe
Handwarmers (2 pr)

Camera
Penknife

MEDICAL/ABLUTION EQUIPMENT

Lip balm
Lip repair
Sunscreen 10 (spray)
Sunscreen 25 (spray)
Paracetamol
Diamox
Immodium
Plasters
Bandage
Antiseptic cream
Facial wipes
Toothbrush
Personal toiletries
Shampoo/washing liquid

Survival tip
The Rough Guides and similar books are good references for information on transport and places to stay, but cannot be relied on for places to eat – the majority of restaurants listed in the pre-2000 editions are closed, out of business.

Accommodation

The following loose classification of accommodation exists in the region:
- *Hotel*: Bathroom en suite, stars awarded by the hotel itself, breakfast always included
- *Hospedaje*: Similar to a hotel, but no single rooms, no room telephones or televisions
- *Hosteria*: No bathrooms en suite
- *Cabaña*: Self-catering accommodation, usually a wooden house
- *Alberque*: Large dormitory-style accommodation, not necessarily including breakfast

Set out below is a non-exhaustive list of hotels where the author has been and stayed. Prices relate to 2003. In the major cities there are many hundreds of other possibilities.

MENDOZA

Electricity is 220V/50Hz, with two-pin bayonet plugs. The post offices are called *correo*, and to make a telephone call the *locotorrio* are inexpensive and efficient.

The unit of currency is the Argentinean peso, but $US are also an acceptable unit of currency. Smaller denomination $US are useful, for it is difficult to obtain change in $US. The peso exchange rate to the dollar has varied over the last few years from parity in 1999, 3 to 1 in 2000, 3.5 to 1 in 2001, 4 to 1 in 2002 to 2.8 to 1 in 2003.

Places to stay
Hotel Provincial, Belgrano 1259.
$17 per night. Clean, small rooms, city centre, main street.
Tel/fax 54.261.4258284, email info@provincialmza.com

Park Suites Aparthotel, Av Mitre 753.
$43 per night, modern hotel, generally busy.
Tel 54.261.4131000

El Portal Suites Aparthotel, Necochea 661.
$US55 per night, per room (2–3 persons). Clean, modern hotel, full of other travellers, particularly those going to Aconcagua.
Tel 54.261.4258733, email reserves@elportalsuites.com.ar

For low-budget travellers the Windsor Hotel is next door to El Portal Suites and charges $US10 for a room for two, and around the corner are the Petit Hotel and the Kapac Hotel. This area of Mendoza is very quiet and is close to restaurants and the permit office.

Hosteling Internacional on Espana 343 (mendoza1@hostels.org.ar), or Hostel Campo Base on Mitre 946 (mendoza2@hostels.org.ar) are alternative low-budget hostels costing less than $US20 for a room.

The Hotel Aconcagua on San Lorenzo 545 is an example of an up-market establishment in the $US100+ bracket (www.hotelaconcagua.com.ar).

Eating out
La Florencia on the corner of Sarmiento and Perú is possibly Mendoza's best restaurant. It is not expensive, and the quality of food excellent. The restaurant has its own ranch that supplies the meat, and there is clear glass between the kitchen and the street, so the food preparation can be seen from the tables outside. Their *bife de chorizo* may rival the best steak you are ever likely to eat.

There are a number of large restaurants in the city where there is a set charge and no limit on how much you eat, such as Las Tinajas on Lavalle 38 and Caro Pepe on Las Heras.

Also on Las Heras at 485 is De un Rincón, a good quality, quiet restaurant. Further along at 596 is the lively Mediterráneo.

On Villanueva between Parque General San Martin and Belgrano there are many restaurants, for example Torcuato, an expensive establishment that serves great food.

Mountain equipment
Three outlets sell and hire mountain equipment, from crampons, double plastic boots, tents, down jackets and sleeping bags to cooking stoves and camping utensils. The rental is approximately 10 per cent of the purchase cost per day, or 25 per cent for 20 days. A credit guarantee is required.

Orviz is located at Juan B. Gusto 536 (close to Inka Expediciones).
Tel 54.261.4251281, email orviz@lanet.com.ar

Pierobon Montaña is at Suipacha 435.
Tel 54.261.4256719, email pierobon@lanet.com.ar

El Refugio Adventure Equipment is at Peatonal Sarmiento 294 in the city centre at Plaza Independencia.
Tel 54.261.423 5615, www.aconcagua6962.com.ar, email el_refugio@fullzero.com.ar

Wineries

Mendoza lies at the heart of the Argentinean wine industry, and it is not far from the city centre to the vineyards. An excellent book entitled *Wine Routes of Argentina* and written by an Australian, Alan Young, living in California, can be ordered direct via ayoung@firstworld.net

The choice of vineyards is enormous. English is spoken at all the larger ones, and wine tours are constantly in progress, though the mornings may be more pleasant. The Weinert Winery is close to Casa Fader. Chandon, Etchart, Trapiche, Finca Flinchman and Norton are other choices with international reputations.

These are some of the big names in Argentinean wine, but some of the smaller vineyards are worth a visit too. They will generally not speak English, but will have a surprisingly varied choice. Although *malbec* is the grape with which Argentina has become synonymous, these smaller vineyards produce wines from such other grapes as *tokay*, *barbera* and *bonarda*. The harsher grape varieties native to Argentina (and ones to be generally avoided) are *criolla grande* and *cereza*.

White-water rafting

The Las Cuevas river, fed by water from the Aconcagua area, becomes the River Mendoza after Punta de Vacas. As it descends into the valley there are centres for water sports, particularly rafting.

The three most prominent companies are Argentina Rafting, Betacourt Rafting and Rios Andinos. Argentina Rafting has its main office in Mendoza on Peatonal Sarmiento 223, tel 54.261.4290029. They will take clients from Mendoza to their Potrerillos centre (near the Vallecitos turn-off). The company also offers trekking, horse trekking and rock climbing. Events are well organised and a weekly programme is set. The Potrerillos centre has a good café.

VALLECITOS

There is only one hostel in Vallecitos, the Ski y Montañas, catering for 40 persons. The bedrooms have bunks, with 4, 6, 8 or 10 per room. There are four bathrooms. The cost is a mere $6 per night for bed, an extra $2 for a limited breakfast, $4 for a large breakfast, and $4 for dinner. Tel 54.261.4236569, email <u>informes@skivallecitos.com</u> and website <u>www.expedicioneselplata.com.ar</u>

LOS PENITENTES AND PUENTE DEL INCA

The Ayelen in Los Penitentes is divided into a hotel and hosteria. Open 365 days a years, the Ayelen's hosteria will charge $US13 for a bunk bed in a 4-person dormitory, whereas the hotel's rate is $US35 per room (3 beds). There is little to choose between the quality of the hotel and the hosteria. Dinner in the Ayelen can be relatively expensive, whereas a meal in the hosteria café is cheaper, quicker and less formal. The Ayelen hotel was given a limited facelift in 2003; its main advantage may be the central heating.

An alternative across the road is the Cruz de Caña, with 70 beds in 3-, 4- and 5-person bedrooms, and in a large dormitory. The cost is $12 per person for bed, breakfast and either dinner or lunch.

In Puente del Inca the Hosteria Puente del Inca has the word 'Hospedaje' over the entrance. It has 92 beds in 3-, 4-, 5- and 6-person rooms, with a bathroom per room. The cost is $14 per night, which is good value; dinner at $5 is also excellent value. Tel 54.26.24.420266, email <u>hpdelinca@yahoo.com.ar</u>

To contact the army hostel, Ejercito Argentina, tel 54.26.24420138, email <u>cacazm8@uspallatadigital.com.ar</u> Contact will have to be in Spanish. The cost per night is $9, including a reasonable breakfast.

SANTIAGO

At the time of writing there are approximately 620 Chilean pesos to the $US. You will be quoted exchange rates from 600 to 640. VAT (or IVA) in Chile is 18 per cent. Tourists are exempt if payments are in $US, but virtually no one is aware of this. Throughout Chile there are ATMs that pay a reasonable rate of exchange.

Electricity is at 220V/50Hz, with two-pronged round-pin plugs.

Places to stay

Along Santiago's main street, the Alameda – Ave Bernardo O'Higgins – there is the imposing structure of Iglesia San Francisco. This is between the metro stations of Universidad de Chile and Santa Lucia. Behind and beside the church there is a range of hotels. Although this is the centre of town, the streets behind Iglesia San

Francisco are bustling during the day with students, but quiet and safe at night. On Paseo Paris there are three hotels: Hotel Paris, Hotel Londres and Hotel Vegas.

Hotel Paris costs $22. It continues to be popular because it is in most guide-books. However, it no longer has any internal courtyard/garden, is cramped and serves a poor breakfast in a tiny room. Best value of the three is Hotel Vegas which, at $36, is perhaps on the high side, but the rooms are spacious and clean, the attention to guests is first class and the breakfast is enormous. Tel 632 2498, fax 632 5084, email info@hotelvegas.net

An alternative hotel location is Baquedano, at the junction of the Alameda and Vicuna Mackenna. This is a very convenient place to stay, and there are a number of hotels.

Hotel Principado is a clean, middle-priced hotel, very conveniently located beside the Baquedano metro. It is on Vicuna Mackenna, costs $US45 for a single room and $US50 for a double, including breakfast. There is a good, inexpensive restaurant next door. A short walk leads into the Bellavista district, where there is a public park, a zoo, and a throbbing nightlife of restaurants and street markets www.hotelesprincipado.com

Nearby on Vicuna Mackenna 47 is Hostel Rio Amazonas. At $22 per night this is exceptional value; tel 562.6719013, email amazona@entelchile.net Hotel Durato on Augustinas is closer to the main shopping areas and even less expensive. www.chile-hotels.com has a long list of other hotels.

Eating out

There are plenty of cafés and bars in the city that serve Western and Chilean food, including a McDonald's on Alameda beside the Universidad de Chile metro. These are open all week, some serving into the early morning. All the restaurants, however, close on Sundays and most are also closed on Saturday evening.

There are four restaurant areas in Santiago: Bellavista, El Bosque Norte, Santa Lucia and Providencia. The Bellavista district under San Cristobal is a walk up from the Baquedano metro station. Alternatively, a taxi ride to the corner of Constitucion and Dardignac will reveal a choice of restaurants in easy reach.

La Bohème is a good-quality French restaurant at Constitucion 124. Their *crevettes bohème* is a chilled prawn cocktail in a tomato sauce. Try the *sauté d'agneau à la biére* (lamb on the bone), and maybe finish with a trio of sorbets.

El Bosque Norte, near Tobalaba metro, has many Western-style bars and restaurants, including an English pub, an Irish pub and a German beer garden. The cuisine is distinctly Western (and so are the prices).

A little further west, in Providencia, between the Alameda and the river, behind Los Leones metro, there are restaurants with a more Chilean flavour.

The Santa Lucia restaurant area is mainly centred on Merced and the streets south of it and between Cerro Santa Lucia and Parque Forestal. On Merced there is a small French restaurant, Les Assassins, on one side of the street and La Terraza de Cerro on the other side. The latter serves excellent fish dishes.

Los Buenos Muchachos is an experience not to be missed in Santiago. This rather large restaurant serves the best steaks while putting on a floorshow of typical Chilean dance and culture. Situated a little away from the city centre on Ricardo Cumming, it is reasonably priced, and therefore very popular, so booking is advisable.

To experience a real piece of Chilean life, go to Mercado Central for a fish lunch. Even if fish is not to your liking the experience is worthwhile. Bring a camera. The restaurants are open (and particularly busy) on Sundays (when other restaurants are closed). The enormous steel structure of Mercado Central is close to Cal y Canto metro, and can seat 800 customers. Around the restaurants are many bustling fish stalls. Dónde Augusto is the largest of the restaurants here, and serves huge portions, so eat the starter before ordering another course. The *paila marina* is a mixed seafood soup that might be more aptly described as a fish stew. Try the conger eel in batter, and do not leave without tasting the *postre of mote con huesillo* (peach in syrup).

Acuario is a small restaurant on Paris 817; it is quiet and serves good food at a very reasonable cost.

For those wanting to sample traditional Chilean cuisine, *pastel de chocho* and *cazuela de ave* are popular in the Santiago area.

If time or energy is not available for wine excursions there are many excellent wine establishments in the city. Try The Wine House on El Bosque Norte, or Vinoteca Isidora on Goyenechan.

Gear shops

There are two shops side-by-side in the El Bosque Norte district, Patagonia Gear and Andesgear, on the corner of Helvecia and Ebro.

La Cumbre will almost certainly have all that the mountaineer needs, and the best quality, but it is rather expensive. This German-owned shop is on Ave Apoquindo 5258, on the left approximately 1km beyond the metro Esc Militar.

Dako Sports are on Ave las Condes 9038, a little out of town. The shop caters for all outdoor sports.

UPPI is a shop selling some Chilean-made gear that is good and inexpensive. They are on Ave Italia 1586, not very accessible.

Foreign embassies

Great Britain	El Bosque Norte 125	3704100
USA	Ave Andres Bello 2800	2322600
Canada	Nueva Tajamar 481, Torre Norte	3629660
Australia	Gertrudis Echeñique 420	2285065
Others	Austria	2234774
	Spain	2352755
	France	2251030
	Germany	4632500
	Holland	2236825
	Norway	2342888
	Czech Republic	2311910
	Switzerland	2634211
	Sweden	2312733

TUPUNGATO

The website www.peakware.com is a source of information on Tupungato. It is a receptacle for personal experiences on the mountain.

Those listed as providing services on Aconcagua are generally available to provide similar services on Tupungato. Andes Mountain Expediciones of Chile have guided treks throughout the summer.

There are two hotels in Tupungato, both on the main street, the Hotel Italia and the Hotel Turismo. The latter has the tourist office in the reception and charges $10.5 per night, or $16 for full board.

There are two hosterias, the Don Romulo (email donromulo@ar.inter.net) and the Refuge of the Condor (tel 54.2622 48 9021).

South American cuisine

Not Spanish

A *bocadillo* may be a French bread sandwich in Spain, but it is a mixed food ball, generally vegetable, in South America. 'Sandwich' is the common term here. A *bocadillo de acelga* is a ball mixture of chopped vegetables, cheese and garlic.

There are no *tapas* (snacks at a bar or before a meal), but you may be served *picadas*, the regional equivalent.

Mantequilla is butter in Spain and in Chile, and *manteca* is lard in Spain, but *manteca* is the more common name in Argentina for butter.

Snacks and starter courses

A common *picada* in a restaurant or café is simply *pan amasado* and *pebre*. *Pan amasado* is home-made bread, generally pitta bread, and *pebre* is a sauce of hot chilli peppers, tomatoes and garlic in olive oil. This will often be placed on the table as an appetiser before a meal. *Matambre arollado* is a paté of vegetables and meat.

By far the most popular snack in South America is an *empanada*. This is similar to an English Cornish pasty – minced meat and chopped potato inside pastry. Variations include some chopped vegetables in the mix. However, the *empanada* has expanded into cheese (*queso*) and even sweet varieties. They are always hot, made and sold on the side of the road, out of insulated carriers at the border, presented as starters at even the smartest of restaurants. The international fast food chain McDonald's serves *empanadas* in Santiago.

Tortas are semi-sweet bread rolls. *Alfajores* are sweet cake sandwiches, usually with chocolate inside. Many sweet cakes and biscuits are made with *dulce de leche*. This mixture of glucose of maize, sugar and milk, is a near obsession in Argentina. It is applied like jam or peanut butter to many foodstuffs – apples, biscuits, and even cheese.

Empanadas *and* pan amasado *being cooked at a roadside café*

Meat dishes

Fish will often be on the menu in Santiago, but virtually never in Mendoza. Here beef is king. *Bife*, pure beef, comes in many cuts and preparations. *Bife de chorizo* is the prime form, simply grilled sirloin, or *châteaubriand*. *Bife de chorizo* is a common term is Argentina, but not quite so universal, except in Santiago, in Chile. How long it is to be grilled for is easy – one quarter (*uno quarto*), half (*medio*), *tres quartos* or *punto*.

Carne is meat. *Asado* is barbecued meat. *Estofado* is a stew. *Porilla* or *porillada* is a popular meal in Argentina. The dish is a portion of three different meats – beef/steak, black pudding (*morcilla*) and sausage (*chorizo*), all grilled. Additional servings of the beef/steak are generally provided at no extra cost.

A *lomito* is a steak sandwich, traditionally in pitta bread, garnished with slices of salad, mayonnaise and tomato sauce. In the cities the pitta bread may be replaced with French bread. A *lomito completo* has a fried egg added to the sandwich. A *chacarero* sandwich is very similar to a *lomito*, but the meat comes in thin, lean strips.

Arollado chancho is rolled pork. *Riñon al Jerez* is kidneys in sherry sauce.

Fish dishes

Sopa surtido de mariscos is a shellfish soup. Fresh fish of trout (*trucha*), hake (*merluza*), sea trout (*corvine*) and salmon (*salmon*) are common in Chilean restaurants. Some specialist restaurants will also have unusual varieties on the menu, such as flounder (*lenguado*), tuna (*atun*), conger eel (*anguila*) and shellfish (*mariscos*).

Desserts

Postre is the Spanish for desert. The most common *postres* are flans, jellies (*gelatine*) and ice-cream (*helado*). *Higos en almíbar* is figs in syrup, whilst *alcayota con nuez* is a syrup of string fruit with nuts.

Drinks

Wine is cheap and plentiful in both countries. Between them Argentina and Chile produce wine using the same range of grape varieties as Europe or North America. They also have their own particular grapes – notably *carmenére* in Chile and *malbec* in Argentina.

The weather is not as temperamental here as in France or other countries, so that particular vintages are not so important. The South Americans virtually always oak their wines, generally in French oak barrels, but the degree of oak ageing is not as high as in Australia or, indeed, Spain.

The *carmanére* vine was brought from France in the 18th century, where it was as popular in Bordeaux as *cabernet sauvignon*. After the phylloxera the vine

Fish dishes being served
at Mercado Central

was never returned to France, because the French had never been able to achieve good yields from the vine. Effectively the *carmanére* grape died out. In the 1990s during DNA testing of Chilean *merlot* grapes it was rediscovered, and in the space of a few years *carmanére* rose from obscurity to become the national grape of Chile. At a wine fair in Santiago in 2003 every wine producer had samples of *carmanére* for tasting. *Pais* is a simple, local wine.

Beer (*cerveza*) in South America nearly always comes in half-litre or 1-litre bottles. Very similar to Western lager, the brand names of Andes and Brahma are popular in Argentina, whilst Castel and Estudo are similar brands in Chile.

In the Potrerillos area the brand name Jerome is available. This beer comes in three flavours – *negra* (black), *roja* (red) and *rubia* (blonde). The *rubia* is very similar to a lager. The *roja* could be likened to an English light ale, whilst the *negra* has a slightly bitter taste.

Pisco sour is a most popular aperitif or cocktail, particularly in Chile. It is a mixture of *pisco* wine, egg white, lemon juice and sugar. *Pisco* wine is made in Chile from *muscatel* grapes and can be purchased in a number of different concentrations.

Chicha is a grape cider, very harsh and high in alcohol content, usually only available in the countryside. In the north *chicha* is a milky beer, made from maize.

Spanish–English

Language necessity
Few ordinary Argentineans speak English, and even fewer Chileans. Those who interface directly with climbers, such as guides, will have a reasonable command of English, but the arrieros, the doctor, the airline official and the bus conductor are unlikely to have any.

On the mountain salutations in Spanish are the norm. For those who are making an unguided expedition, a reasonable command of Spanish is recommended, if not essential. Even for those with hired guides there will be many occasions when a basic knowledge of Spanish is desirable.

South American Spanish
South American Spanish has some dissimilarities to European Spanish, for instance, how to pronounce words including the letter 'c'. In South America the language is softer, less harsh than in Spain. Argentinean Spanish is different from Chilean Spanish, but the Spanish of Mendoza is more like Chilean Spanish. Chileans speak very fast. They regularly drop the 's' from the ends of words, and use many slang words and words with their origin in the native Indian. *Buenos dias*, for example, will be heard as *Bueno dia*.

Survival tip

For those with little Spanish perhaps the most important difference from English, and the feature that is the source of most mispronunciations, is the letter 'V'. This is pronounced as 'B'.

The basics of Spanish, however, hold. These will be found in phrasebooks and dictionaries, and include:

H	is always silent
J	is pronounced similar to 'ch' in Scottish loch
LL	is pronounced like 'y' in yellow
Ñ	is pronounced like 'ni' in onion
V	is pronounced like 'b'

Listed below are some of the names and common words or expressions that may be encountered, pronounced in the Mendoza-Chile style, with their English equivalent.

Proper nouns

Words ending in *agua* such as Aconcagua and Rancagua are pronounced 'aawaa'. There are a few differing interpretations of the origin of Aconcagua. Some postulate that it is derived from the Quecha language:

Akun	Summit
Ka	Other
Agua	Fearful (others suggest it is 'Aymara' and means sentinel of stone)
Alameda	Promenade
Argentina	The 'g' is pronounced as in 'get'
Quebrada	Deep stream
Casa del Cura	House of the priest
Casa de Piedra	House of stone
Cerro Mirador	Mountain viewpoint
Cristo Redentor	Christ the Redeemer
Chile	Pronounced 'chiily'
Las Cuevas	The caves
Cordón del Plata	The string or line of the silver
Cresto del Viento	Windy crest
Ejercito	Army
Estancia	Ranch or farm

La Hoyada	The pit, pothole
Mendoza	Pronounce the 'z' as in English
Lomas Blancas	White hills
La Olla	The cooking pot
Pabellón	Pavilion, tent
Penitentes	Standing icicles
Plata	Silver
Plomo	Lead (metal)
Portezuelo del Fraile	Col of the friar
Punta de Vacas	The point of (the river of) cows
Puente del Inca	Bridge of the Incas
Pampa de Leñas	Plain where there is firewood
Rocas Blancas	White rocks
El Salto	The jump or leap
Valle de Las Vacas	Valley of the cows
Vallecitos	Little valleys (Buy-ay-see-tos)

Salutations

Hola	Hello
Buenos días	Good day/morning
Buenas tardes	Good afternoon
Buenas noches	Good evening/night
Adíos	Goodbye
Hasta luego	See you later
Cómo estás?	How are you?
Muy bien, y tú?	Very good, and you?
Buen provecho	*Bon appétit*

Numbers

0	Cero
1	Uno
2	Dos
3	Tres
4	Cuatro
5	Cinco
6	Seis
7	Siete
8	Ocho
9	Nueve
10	Diez

11	Once
12	Doce
13	Trece
14	Catorce
15	Quince
16	Dieciséis
17	Diecisiete
18	Dieciocho
19	Diecinueve
20	Veinte
21	Veintiuno
29	Veintinueve
30	Treinta
32	Treinta y dos
40	Cuarenta
50	Cincuenta
60	Sesanta
70	Setenta
80	Ochenta
90	Noventa
100	Cien
110	Ciento diez
200	Doscientos
1000	Mil
2000	Dos mil
Million	Un millón

Alphabet

A	Aconcagua	a
B	Bilbao	be
C	Carmen	ce
Ch	Champiñon	che
D	Deportivo	de
E	Español	e
F	Francia	efe
G	Go	khe
H	Hasta	aache
I	Isabel	ee
J	José	khota
K	Kilo	ka

L	Londres	ele
Ll	Tortilla	elye
M	Metro	eme
N	Noches	ene
O	Otro	o
P	Puente	pe
Q	Quisiera	koo
R	Río	ere
S	Sábado	ese
T	Tardes	te
U	Uno	oo
V	Viento	oobay
W	Washington	oobay doblay
X	Taxi	ekees
Y	Paraquay	eegriayge
Z	Zeta	theta

Days

Monday	Lunes
Tuesday	Martes
Wednesday	Miércoles
Thursday	Jueves
Friday	Viernes
Saturday	Sábado
Sunday	Domingo

Months

January	Enero
February	Febrero
March	Marzo
April	Abril
May	Mayo
June	Junio
July	Julio
August	Agosto
September	Septiembre
October	Octubre
November	Noviembre
December	Diciembre

Seasons

Spring	La Primavera
Summer	El Verano
Autumn	El Otoño
Winter	El Invierno

Colours

Black	negro
Blue	azul
Brown	marrón
Cream	crema
Gold	dorado
Green	verde
Grey	gris
Orange	naranja
Red	rojo
Silver	plateado
White	blanco
Yellow	amarillo

Shapes

Big	grande
Fat	gordo/a
Flat	llano/a
Long	largo/a
Narrow	estrecho/a
Round	redondo/a
Small	pequeño/a
Tall	alto/a
Thin	delgado
Tiny	pequeñito

Food

Apple	la manzana (manthana)
Banana	la plátano
Biscuits	las galletas
Bread	el pan
Bread roll	el panecillo
Butter	la mantequilla (manteca in Argentina)
Cheese	el queso

Chicken	el pollo
Chips	las papas fritas
Eggs	los huevos
Garlic	la ajo
Ham	el jamón
Honey	la miel
Jam	la marmelada
Marmalade	la marmelada de naranja
Milk	la leche
Mushrooms	los champiñones
Mustard	la mostaza
Onion	la cebolla
Pepper	la pimienta
Potatoes	las papas
Prawns	las gambas
Rice	el arroz
Salt	la sal
Steak	el bistec or bife
Stew	el estofado
A portion of . . .	una ración de . . .
Breakfast	el desayuno
Lunch	la comida, el almuerzo
Dinner	la cena
Plate	el plato
Boiled	hervido
Fried	frito
Grilled	a la parrilla
Roast	asado
Scrambled	revueltos
Stewed	cocido, guisado
Rare	poco hecho, uno quarto
Medium	normal, medio
Well done	bien hecho, a punto
Menu	la carta
Set menu	el menu del día

Words particular to mountains

Air bed	Colchón neumático
Altitude, height	Altura

Blister	Ampolla
Bottle	Botella
Campsite Camping,	lugar de campamento
Cliff	Precipicio
Cloud	Nube
Compass	Brújula
Danger	Peligro
East	Este
Fingers	Dedos
Foot	Pie
Frost	Helada
Frozen	Congelado
Headache	Dolor de cabeza
Helmet	Casco
Keep straight ahead	Siga derecho
Loose stones, scree	Acarreo
Mist	Neblina
Mountain range	Cordillera
Mountain	Cerro
North	Norte
Rock climbing	Rappel
Shelter	Refugio
Sleeping bag	Saco de dormir
Slippery	Resbaladizo
Slowly	Despacio
Snow	Nieve
South	Sur
Sports shop	Tienda de deportes
Summit	Cima, cumbre
Sunglasses	Gafas de sol
Suntan oil	Aceite bronceador
Toe	Dedo del pie
Toilet	Excusado
Toilets	Aseos
Torch	Linterna
Trek	Caminata
Trekking on horseback	Cabalgata
West	Oeste

INDEX

LISTING OF CICERONE GUIDES

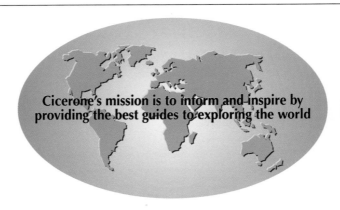

Cicerone's mission is to inform and inspire by providing the best guides to exploring the world

Since its foundation over 30 years ago, Cicerone has specialised in publishing guidebooks and has built a reputation for quality and reliability. It now publishes nearly 300 guides to the major destinations for outdoor enthusiasts, including Europe, UK and the rest of the world.

Written by leading and committed specialists, Cicerone guides are recognised as the most authoritative. They are full of information, maps and illustrations so that the user can plan and complete a successful and safe trip or expedition – be it a long face climb, a walk over Lakeland fells, an alpine traverse, a Himalayan trek or a ramble in the countryside.

With a thorough introduction to assist planning, clear diagrams, maps and colour photographs to illustrate the terrain and route, and accurate and detailed text, Cicerone guides are designed for ease of use and access to the information.

If the facts on the ground change, or there is any aspect of a guide that you think we can improve, we are always delighted to hear from you.

Cicerone Press
2 Police Square Milnthorpe Cumbria LA7 7PY
Tel:01539 562 069   Fax:01539 563 417
e-mail:info@cicerone.co.uk   web:www.cicerone.co.uk